Celtic Mythology

Tales From the Celtic Pantheon

Adam Andino

Table of Contents

Introduction:

A Brief History of Celtic Mythology

Enya, the top-selling solo Irish singer of all time, once said about the ancient mythology of the Celtic pantheon: "There's something about Celtic mythology which is deep in the soul." While she is most known for her modern Celtic folk songs, some of the inspiration to write such compositions is rooted in Celtic mythology. While many of the deities are comparable to others such as the Roman and Norse mythologies, many of the Celtic myths are vastly different from the others. The pantheon and the creatures themselves are sometimes the complete opposite of what one would expect.

The pantheon of the Celts is little known due to its oral traditions, war with Rome, and the culture's migratory past. Similar to the Norse pantheon, many of the stories and legends have been erased from history. The Celts often lacked literacy, so their stories were passed down orally throughout the generations.

The Celts

As mentioned previously, the lack of information derives from three main facets of change: the war with Rome, oral traditions, and the need to migrate. The Celtic people, in a nutshell, are from the regions which are now Wales, Scotland, Ireland, France, and Spain, and even expanded as far as Turkey. The people in each region had their unique culture and language, but their polytheistic religions and deities often overlapped. Celtic dialects still exist, most notably in Wales and Ireland; some Scottish and Irish still speak versions of Gaelic, and some of the people from Wales can speak Welsh.

The Celtic people started their civilization as early as 1200 BCE during the Iron Age, when humans discovered how to construct tools out of metal. They were craftsmen of bronze, gold, and mercury with intricate designs of spirals on their jewelry and weapons. They branched from Europe to Turkey, even going as far south as Egypt. There is conjecture that some of the Celts were even mercenaries for the Egyptian queen Cleopatra.

They remained in tribes until Julius Caesar of the Roman Empire waged war on their culture around 70 BCE. During this bitter war, he was also the first to document the Celtic culture. He deemed them "Gauls," which also translated to "barbaric". The Gauls were the people located in what is now known as France.

The Loss of a Culture

Even though Julius Caesar attempted to rid the Roman Empire of the Gauls, the culture remained steadfast. The Romans and even the Greeks admired the Celts in battle, which prompted many writers of the era and beyond to study and document them. As a result, a few documents about the Celtic cultures and peoples were written during this war. However, this admiration of the Celts would not last. While the Roman Empire is a contender in the almost-extinction of the Celts, there were other factors, as well.

The Druids

The druids were a religious faction of the Celtic people and were considered the wisest. They believed in reincarnation and worshipped many deities of their polytheistic religion. Similar to other pantheons of antiquity, the Celts worshipped deities based on nature, such as the sun and moon, rivers and lakes, and agriculture. The druids, who acted as healers and religious figureheads, believed they were able to tell the future through bird formations, dream interpretations, and meditation. Men and women were equally welcome in their establishments and were also involved in education and their justice system.

The druids believed that their traditions didn't need to be written down, but instead should be passed down through oral means. They often forbade written texts to preserve their oral traditions. As a result, their civilization lacked documentation of religious and cultural ceremonies and procedures. The few remnants of their culture were preserved in caves in the Alps written in their language, Caesar's accounts, and the medieval accounts of Christian priests.

The Introduction of Christianity

The introduction of Christianity was also a culprit in the downfall of the Celtic people and their pantheon. After Christianity became the dominant religion in Rome and its empire, the forces behind the Crusades deemed polytheism unholy and conquered the many Celtic peoples. In 432 CE, Christianity was forced upon the Celtic people in Britain by the introduction of Saint Patrick. Many of the former deities were assimilated into the Christian faith as saints, and their practices were assimilated into Christianity.

However, this new religion was met with resistance. As a response, the Catholics ordered the eradication of the druids through mass killings. This tumultuous time led to the annihilation of the polytheistic religion. Traces of the culture remain to this day with the reintroduction of speaking the ancient Celtic languages such as Gaelic and Welsh, and even through religious symbols. The Celtic cross and the shamrock of Ireland represent this turbulent past and the traces of their culture. Some of the stories and legends are still told in Ireland to this day.

Daily Living for the Celts

The Celtic people were similar to the Nordic people in how they went about their daily lives. Although they were not sea-faring people, they migrated to different parts of Northern Europe. They lived in tribes within a village surrounded by stone walls and used that same stone to build their houses. The roofs were crafted into cones constructed with reeds and straw. Their craftsmanship also included metalwork such as jewelry and weaponry.

Renowned for their combat and horseback riding skills, the Celts were brave and fierce warriors. It was documented that the warriors also rode into battle in the nude, possibly to intimidate their enemies. Some surviving texts claim that they also kept the heads of their enemies as trophies. However, their fighting was often unorganized warfare, which was later rendered obsolete in the presence of the Roman armies.

Not all Celtic men were warriors. Other professions included craftsmanship, blacksmithing, agriculture, druidism, and even poetry. Bards were responsible for memorizing and reciting the generational stories and legends of their people. Each profession was no more significant than the others, and men had the right to choose.

Women, in addition, were not confined to adopting a housekeeper role. Women could hold the same positions as men, whether the roles were warrior, religious figure, or even political leader. They had the same rights as men, which included divorce and having assets in their name.

The Religious Customs of the Celts

The Celtic people had a few religious customs in their culture. In addition to worshipping deities, they also considered parts of nature to be sacred. Oak trees and forests are an example of their reverence for the natural world. They worshipped nature as if it was a being in itself. Rituals of both religious and political importance were performed in forests.

Part of the rituals included animal and human sacrifices to appease certain deities. There is evidence of both human and animal sacrifices in sacred places such as wetlands and forests. They also burned effigies created with straw and with humans inside as either appeasement of the gods or as a form of justice. The Celtic people also sacrificed weapons to the sea god by throwing them into bogs, rivers, and other bodies of water.

While there were horrifying accounts of these activities, the Celts also worshipped the gods through festivals. In May, they celebrated Beltane, now known as Midsummer's Eve, which was a day for dance and song. This festival marked the warmer months of spring and summer, which then encouraged agriculture.

Samhain was on the last day of October and the first of November when they celebrated the dead, and even wore costumes and masks. Samhain was the decline of the sun and therefore, the barrier between reality and the Overworld thinned. It was believed that during this time, ancestors and spirits could make contact with the living. However, there were also evil spirits. To protect themselves from these harmful spirits, the Celts donned costumes and masks as a disguise to prevent harm. This practice is one of the ancestors of the modern-day celebration of Halloween.

Despite not having a lot of written texts, the Celtic people did have myths and legends that fortunately haven't been lost to time. Some of the stories are convoluted and incomplete due to a lack of written text. Some deities are even in this category as well, with little known about the religion, myths, and legends as a whole. The mystery of these deities and stories has led archaeologists and fans of mythology to make discoveries of the almost-lost civilization and its unique perspective on religion. In the next chapter, the gods and goddesses will receive their proper introduction.

Chapter 1: 11 Main Gods and Goddesses

In contrast to other mythologies such as Greek, Roman, and Egyptian, the Celtic pantheon is incomplete. This mythology is similar to the Norse pantheon with its incomplete myths. However, there has been somewhat of a resurrection of learning more about the Celtic pantheon. Celtic music from Ireland from a cappella groups such as Anuna and Celtic Women, and even Swiss metal bands including Eluveitie, all perform songs about Celtic myths. These bands sing both English as well as Celtic lyrics. Anuna and Celtic Women specialize in Irish Celtic, while Eluveitie specializes in the mythology and language of ancient Gaul. Some of Eluveitie's songs refer to the deities themselves as song titles, with intricate use of instruments and heavy metal moments, while simultaneously recounting memories of life back then. Due to the popularity of these groups, the Celtic renewal of learning about ancestry and forgotten history is at its peak.

While there is a current resurrection of the Celtic pantheon, there is still little representation of the gods themselves. Because each tribe had its own language, and therefore its own gods and goddesses, some of the deities represent the same being but with a different name. In total, there are about 400 separate deities within the Celtic pantheon as a whole, including those of individual tribes. However, in this chapter, only the common ones will be discussed. Below are the main gods and goddesses in alphabetical order; in parentheses are their names in other Celtic languages.

Aengus (Aengus Óg, Óengus): God of Love

Aengus was the god of youth, love, poetry, and summer. He was born out of an affair between his father, the Dagda, and the Dagda's mistress Boann, who was also one of the river goddesses. In response to his mistress falling pregnant, the Dagda placed a spell on his son to speed up the time from conception to birth, resulting in Aengus's eternal youth. He was often portrayed with birds flying around him, representing his kisses and love. Aengus and his lover often appeared as swans encircling each other, a myth that is further explained in Chapter 3.

Belenos (Bel, Belus): God of Healing

Also known as the Latinized "Belenus," this deity was the god of healing, medicine, the sun, spring festivals, agriculture, and fire. The god of healing was once married to Danu, goddess of wisdom and fertility, but has no other known family relationships. His abilities closely mirror Apollo, the god of the sun, agriculture, and healing. He is often portrayed with horses and lightning bolts used to disrupt conflicts. While some of the other deities were only represented in a singular tribe, there is evidence that the worship of Belenos extended from Italy to Britain.

Brigid (Brigit): Goddess of Fertility

Brigid was the daughter of the Dagda and was married to Bres, a god of fertility and a tyrant. She was also the mother of Ruadan, a priest known for his prophecies in 600 CE, and later became one of the Twelve Apostles of Ireland. Brigid was a beloved goddess, as she was the goddess of healing, smithing, fire, poetry, passion, fertility, and motherhood. According to historian N.S. Gill, because Brigid was so highly revered, she was introduced into sainthood after the Catholics conquered the Celts. Often, she was compared to the Roman goddesses Minerva and Vesta.

Cernunnos: God of Wildlife

Not much is known about the god of fertility, grain, nature, wealth, the Underworld, and wildlife: Cernunnos. If not for the archaeological findings of ancient Celtic art, Cernunnos most likely would not exist in the pantheon as we know it today. Also known as the Horned God, Cernunnos was often associated with horned animals such as stags and bulls. In ancient art, he was often portrayed as a figure sitting cross-legged with massive horns attached to his head. His relationship with the other gods is unknown, but it has been discovered that the god is reborn every winter solstice and dies during the summer solstice. Cernunnos was widely revered by the druids. It is also believed that Cernunnos is the inspiration for Satan's horned appearance in Christianity.

The Dagda (Sucellos): King of the Gods

The Dagda was the king of the gods. While many main gods in other mythologies such as Roman, Norse, and Greek portrayed their god-kings as cruel and pugnacious, the Dagda was the opposite. He was known as "the good god" and ruled over knowledge, fertility, reincarnation, death, rebirth, artisans, agriculture, protection, music, and many other facets. He was essentially the master of all trades and the protector of the lands. He was often portrayed as a jolly, fun-loving god with a harp by his side instilled with magical qualities to change both emotions and the seasons. In his possession, he also had a cauldron that never ran empty and was dually equipped with a magical staff and mace for resurrection and death, respectively.

The Dagda was the father of Aengus, Aed, Brigid, Cermait, Danu, and Bobd Derg and was married to the Morrigan. There are many tales and myths revolving around the Dagda and his family, which will be further explored in later chapters.

Danu (Annan, Anu): Goddess of Wisdom and Death

The ancient Celts deemed Danu to be the Mother Goddess, not because she was the wife of the Dagda, but instead because of what she represented. Danu was the goddess of the earth, weather conditions, fertility, death, and wisdom. She was often depicted as battle-ready with a raven on her shoulder, symbolizing her reign over death and wisdom. As a protector of the lands, she was worshipped based on her wisdom in battle. In addition to her role in death and war, she also brought about life and prosperity.

Danu was the daughter of the Dagda and the wife of both Belenos, the god of healing, and the god of the sea, Beli. Whether she had children is a mystery. However, it could be assumed she considered the Celts her children due to her high reverence. Scholars believe that her influence over Celtic culture was responsible for the naming of the Danube River that flows through Europe.

Epona: Patroness of Horses

Epona may be the most recognizable deity by name and her association with horses in particular. Often in the *Legend of Zelda* video game series, one of Link's famous companions is his horse, Epona. Epona in Celtic mythology, however, is more than a companion. She reigned over fertility, agriculture, calvary, horses, mules, donkeys, and oxen. In early texts and illustrations of her, Epona was never depicted in her human form, but instead as either a horse or a mule. However, once she was indoctrinated into Roman mythology due to her admiration from the Roman cavalry, she posed in her human form either on a chariot or on a throne between two horses. Just as with many of the deities in Celtic mythology, it is unknown if she had any familial relationships with the other deities.

Lugh (Lugus, Lamfhada, Luga): The God of Kings

Lugh was the god of kings, justice, the sun, trickery, leadership, and craftsmanship. He was one of the most prominent gods the Celts worshipped, due to his impressive intelligence and skills in battle. He was the object of many myths, including the execution of the one-eyed Balor. The Celts believed he wielded a magical spear against his enemies with superior accuracy to men. Other myths decreed that he possessed the ability to shapeshift into other identities and forms.

According to the myth, Lugh was the father of the most prominent demigod named Cu Chulainn. He often used his trickery to obtain wives and lovers, in addition to his love for games and revenge. One myth about his birth will be covered in Chapter 4.

Manannan (Manannan mac Lir): God of the Sea

Manannan was the god of the sea and guardian of the Overworld, the Celtic pantheon's version of heaven or Elysium. Common stories revolve around Manannan and his children, especially his foster child Aengus and his daughter Niamh. Some sources believe that his wife was Fand, an aquatic deity, or Aine. In some texts, Aine is believed to be his daughter. The father of Manannan was the ocean god Lir.

The Morrigan: Goddess of War

The Morrigan, also known as the Phantom Queen, was the goddess of war, death, prophecy, and fate. She was one of the most fearsome goddesses in the Celtic pantheon, often shapeshifting into other forms. Her other forms consisted of a weak, frail old woman; a raven or crow; a washer of blood-stained armor; and a wolf. It was believed that, when a warrior spotted a crow on the battlefield, their death was near. One of the myths about the Dagda and the Phantom Queen revolve around the prophecy of his death, which will be explained in more detail in Chapter 5.

The Morrigan was often affiliated with a trifecta of goddesses who also went by her name. In some stories, she could either be portrayed as a singular goddess or part of the trifecta with her sisters Nemain, Badb, and Macha. She was also married to the king of the gods himself, the Dagda.

Taranis: God of Thunder

Taranis was the god of thunder, storms, and extreme weather. Taranis often was portrayed with a lightning bolt in his fist while riding a chariot, an image mirroring both Thor of Norse mythology and Zeus of Greek mythology. What set him apart, however, was the often brutal rituals that took place under his name. These rituals also included two other gods: Esus, equivalent to the Roman god Mars, and Teutates, god of the tribe. The triumvirate of these gods often demanded human sacrifice, according to Caesar and later Christian monks set to vilify the polytheistic religion.

There has been evidence that human sacrifice, whether it was under an altar or burning effigies filled with living people, was a common practice to appease Taranis. He was considered one of the protectors of the land and was feared by his cult. Those who believed in Taranis expanded from Ireland to Spain and France with archaeological findings of wheels, one of his symbols. The wheel represented mobility, as well as the quick formation of severe weather.

Conclusion

The gods and goddesses of the Celtic pantheon all played an integral role in the intricacies of life for the Celts. Based on what the gods mostly represented, it was clear that the Celtic people valued fertility and agriculture more so than any other trait. Due to the lack of texts for us to fully understand the complexities of this mythology, its mystery still intrigues many to this day. From video game characters to songs written in ancient Celtic, the memories of the distant past have been resurrected. However, one of the inspirations for an entire genre of fantasy and horror lies in the creatures, demigods, and heroes of the ancient Celtic pantheon.

Chapter 2: Creatures and Characters of the Celtic Pantheon

While it may be tempting to picture the legends of King Arthur and his infamous journey, the Celtic pantheon predates the Arthurian legends. The Celtic pantheon can be seen as the forefather of legends in magical creatures and mystical places with its myths and legends heavily based on the supernatural and fantastic. The creatures ranged from harmless fun to horrifying monsters. The remnants of the Celtic pantheon exist to this day, continuing to inspire new creators and storytellers with its collection of monsters.

Creatures and Monsters

Despite its lack of written texts, Celtic mythology still has a vast richness of unique and horrifying creatures to add to the human imagination. These creatures ranged from harmless nuisances to terrifying monsters. Many of the supernatural creatures we know of today originated from the Celtic pantheon.

Balor

According to legend, there was a realm that many of the supernatural creatures called home. These supernatural creatures were known as the Fomorians, with Balor as their leader. They were said to have lived in the dark depths of lakes and seas. They often wreaked havoc on mortals and the gods themselves.

It was written that Balor had one evil eye and was often portrayed as a giant—equivalent to the cyclops in Greek and Roman mythologies. His one evil eye possessed the power to kill anyone who looked upon it, so he often had it shut. In many of the Celtic myths, the great king perished in a battle at the hand of his grandson, who was believed by scholars to be Lugh himself.

Banshee

The banshee was a common creature whose screech warned mortals of impending death. This monster was quite common among Irish folktales and was even the inspiration for many horror stories. Banshees were often depicted as ghoulish maidens or elderly women whose bone-chilling shrieks warned mortals of their loved ones' future painful demises. Depending on the myth, these shrieking ghouls may've been adorned in a white dress or a gray or black hooded cloak. No matter in what manner she appeared, her bone-chilling wails foretold an inevitable death.

Caorthannach

Also known as the fire-spitter, Caorthannach was a female serpentine demon who fought Saint Patrick. She was believed by some to be the devil's mother. Saint Patrick pursued her from the top of Croagh Patrick after she escaped his attempt to expel all demonic serpents into the sea. She poisoned all forms of drinking water during the pursuit while spitting fire at him, but Patrick did not drink until he cast her into the ocean to drown with the rest.

Dearg-Due

Before Brahm Stoker's Dracula, loosely based on Vlad the Impaler, there was a more prominent vampire in Celtic folklore, specifically in Ireland. The Dearg-Due was a beautiful female demon who lured men to their deaths and drained them of blood. Similar to Dracula, who preyed on women, Dearg-Due preyed on mortal men.

The original Dearg-Due was the story of a wealthy, beautiful, young maiden who fell madly in love with a peasant against her father's wishes. As a result, her father punished her by forcing her to marry another in an arranged marriage. However, there was consistent abuse, leading to her death. As a result, she vowed to take revenge on men from beyond the veil.

Dullahan

Another common creature in today's world took inspiration from the Celtic monster known as the Headless Horseman. Riding on a black horse with blazing ember eyes and clothed with a black cape, he was the harbinger of death and was unafraid to harm innocent bystanders when he rode into the villages. Dullahan carried his head under one arm and whipped his steed, as well as onlookers, with a human spine.

Legend claims that, when he rode into a village, death was soon to follow. Once someone heard their name being called, it was instant death for them. When the death happened, he would raise his head to watch the show. In addition to the banshee, the pair would often appear together and foretold the deaths of many.

Giants

Many of the surviving common myths revolve around giants. Most of the time, the fearsome giants were often in between the hero and their goals or the women they loved. As a result, these obstacles were almost insurmountable in both size and strength. Outside influences, such as Greek and Roman myths, can be compared to the giants in Celtic myths as well.

Fairies

Another common creature of the Celtic pantheon is one of the most prominent fantastical creatures to date. Fairies are omnipresent in media ranging from Disney films to video games and fantasy novels. While it may appear that fairies were often guides, in Celtic mythology, they were known for playing tricks on mortals or leading weary travelers away from their destinations. They were human-like in form and experienced emotions as humans do, but they were endowed with supernatural gifts and powers. They were also depicted in various sizes, ranging from the smallest creature to the size of a human. Fairies, or Fae, often were arranged into two main categories: Unseelie and Seelie.

The Unseelie fae held darkness within them. Most of the time, the Unseelie fae, such as gnomes, played tricks on humans for fun. There were some, however, who were synonymous with demons such as goblins. Throughout history, these types of fairies were believed to be fallen and demoted angels of Christianity, spirits of the dead, or simply demons.

The Seelie fae, in contrast, were helpful and joyful creatures, similar to the fairies depicted in popular culture today. This category of fairy included sprites, wisps, and ethereal spirits who guided the heroes on their journey. The Seelie fae also played harmless pranks on humans. If a fairy was offended, however, it posed a threat in order to protect its realm.

Leprechauns

The leprechaun is a staple in Irish culture, both currently and in the past. The little men donned in green with orange beards carried a four-leafed clover, a symbol of luck. Leprechauns were solitary supernatural beings who often took pleasure in causing mischief. Some scholars believe that leprechauns are considered fairies, but their solitary lifestyles contradict this theory. In later years, the leprechauns were known for their shoemaking and habit of hiding a pot of gold at the end of a rainbow. It was also widely believed that if someone caught a leprechaun, he would grant them three wishes.

The Questing Beast

This ancient beast was a chimera that often struck fear into the hearts of men. The Questing Beast was represented by the head of a serpent, the body of a leopard, the haunches of a lion, and the hooves of a massive deer. This creature often preyed upon warriors and knights during the legends of Arthur. It was claimed that the creature was quick to strike with a battle cry that sounded like 30 wolves howling simultaneously.

Sluagh

The Sluagh were the Celtic ghosts of their pantheon. They were considered sinners who were trapped between the worlds of the living and the dead. Their souls roamed the earth because neither heaven nor hell wanted them; in their rage and grief at their circumstance, the Sluagh stole the souls from the living. Some Irish families would keep their west-facing windows shut at all times to keep the Sluagh out of their homes. However, it was common practice for the Sluagh to rapture any onlooking soul due to their anger at their fate.

A Demigod and a Hero

One of the tragedies of the lost pantheon is that there are so few stories and myths revolving around heroes and demigods. More complete mythologies have the luxury of many myths with demigods, but the Celtic pantheon lacks in this regard. Most of the stories have been lost to time as the many different cultures of the Celts went extinct. Caesar once wrote that the Gauls did have, for example, a creation myth, but what remains are fragments that cannot be pieced together. The same is true for demigods and heroes.

Through traditional oral storytelling, two figures still remain in Irish folklore today; unfortunately, other heroes from the numerous tribes scattered throughout Europe vanished once the Celts were forcefully converted to Catholicism. Despite this conversion, however, the Irish still spoke of tales of the great Cu Chulainn and Finn mac Cumhaill.

The Four Cycles of Mythology

The Celtic pantheon had four different cycles of mythology in which all the stories transpired. Each cycle was a blip in time, ranging from 2000 BCE to 1400 CE, that had its own forms of magic and intrigue. The names of these cycles were: The Invasions Cycle, The Ulster Cycle, The Fenian Cycle, and The Cycle of Kings.

Cu Chulainn

Cu Chulainn was part of the Ulster Cycle of mythology, which encompassed the tales of Uliad, a kingdom with a powerful king named Conchobar mac Nessa. Cu Chulainn was believed to be the son of the sun god Lugh and a mortal woman by the name of Deichtine. There are several stories revolving around his birth, each more scandalous than the last. He was born with the name Setanta, and when he was about five years old, he saved one of his teachers from an enemy's savage hound. As a result, his name was henceforth Cu Chulainn, or "the hound of Culann." Cu Chulainn was a fearsome warrior in battle, most notably for his berserk ability. While in this berserk mode, it was impossible for him to determine friend from foe.

Cu Chulainn achieved legendary status through his many skills in battle and the life he had lived. From accidentally killing his own son, to his many lovers, to his death, Cu Chulainn was a man of intrigue and had many adventures. The stories that involve such a figure in mythology will be explored in Chapter 6.

Finn mac Cumhaill

Finn mac Cumhaill was a hero known for his skills in battle and for using his intelligence to gain the upper hand in other stories. He was part of the Fenian Cycle, whose stories mainly revolved around him. He was largely based on a historical figure in the third century CE and has cemented his status as a legend within the Irish myths. The stories were narrated by his son Oison, a poet.

The Fenian Cycle of mythology chronicles the life of Finn mac Cumhaill. Myths such as the Salmon of Knowledge and the creation of the Giant's Causeway in Ireland were some of the most famous, telling of his powerful knowledge and skillful battle techniques. The description of the hero said he was as tall as a giant and had a magical thumb which provided him with wisdom and knowledge.

Conclusion

The mythical creatures and legends of the Celtic pantheon were remarkable in their ability to inspire future creatives. The monsters were terrifying, and the heroes demanded respect and admiration. The creatures ranged from guiding spirits and nuisances to deadly monsters which created chaos for the heroes of legend and common mortals alike. These creatures, especially those imbued with magical elements, were only part of the myths encompassing the Celtic pantheon. For the rest of this book, the tales surrounding some of these creatures, heroes, and deities will be explored in further detail.

Chapter 3: The Myths of Aengus

Like other mythologies, Celtic mythology often was imbued with themes of love/lust, a quest for power, or saving family members from a fierce foe. The myths in the coming chapters are no exception. Violence, bloodshed, and deception are omnipresent within the myths of Aengus, including his birth and the reason behind his shapeshifting into a swan.

The Product of an Affair

The creation of Aengus was a myth wrapped in deceit from both his father, the Dagda, and his mother, Boann, a goddess of the River Boyne. Boann was married to Elcmar, who was a steward to Dagda. Boann had deep romantic feelings for the Dagda, which were then consummated one night. Some sources claimed that the Dagda visited her in a dream, while others claim that he visited her in person. No matter how it happened, the conception of Aengus was inevitable. In order to consummate their feelings for one another, the Dagda sent Elcmar away on an errand.

Holding the Sun in Place

After it was discovered a child had been conceived, the Dagda used his powers to control the passing of time. In order to hide the illegitimate child from Elcmar, the Dagda's solution was to hold the sun in place until the child was born. For nine months, the Dagda held the sun in place to fool Elcmar, and everyone else, into thinking that only one day had passed.

While Elcmar was away, the Dagda ensured the steward was not uncomfortable. He managed to dispel thirst, hunger, and even darkness from Elcmar, fooling him into believing only one day had passed. Meanwhile, the child grew inside Boann's womb until his birth. Boann named her child Aengus and gave him to the Dagda, who hid him safely away from vengeance in case Elcmar ever found out about his wife's affair and the resulting child.

The Dagda entrusted the child to Midir, one of his sons, to play the role of a father figure. With each passing day, Aengus grew cleverer with his wordplay, which would set him up for future successes in battles of wit. The child grew into a handsome young man who never aged. His immortality was believed to be the result of the Dagda holding the sun in place while he was in the womb.

Reclaim the Castle

It is unclear when Aengus discovered his true lineage, but it was sometime after he was of age. It is speculated that this discovery could have been from his foster father and wife Fuamnach, who are both present in a later myth. After this discovery, Aengus tricked his stepfather into reclaiming his rightful home.

Once he learned the truth of his birth, Aengus sought the Dagda and demanded he give him land, just as he had recently done for his other children. The Dagda refused and instead convinced his son to steal the home of Elcmar at Bru na Boinne.

Aengus, with his slippery tongue, knocked on the door at Bru na Boinne, which revealed Elcmar. Aengus asked for an overnight stay inside the home. Due to the emphasis placed on hospitality in the ancient Celtic world, Elcmar agreed he could stay the night.

Laa ocus aidce. "A day and night." When these words were spoken in the old Irish tongue, they can also be misconstrued to mean "all days and all nights". Aengus planned for these words to be used in this context. Aengus's clever play on words proceeded to confuse and humiliate Elcmar further when it was decreed that Elcmar must give up his lands to the son of his wife's affair.

Alternate Myth

It was also speculated that Aengus used this trick on the Dagda himself in order to reclaim his rightful place. Instead of going to Elcmar's home at Bru na Boinne, some stories claim that the Dagda's residence was at this location. Enraged that his father refused to give him land while his siblings received theirs, Aengus played this exact trick on the Dagda, which forced the god of kings to give this same land to his son.

The Wooing of Etain

The Wooing of Etain was one of the most complete myths in the Invasion Cycle of Celtic mythology. The Invasion Cycle was part of the wars between various supernatural beings—gods and creatures alike—who fought to claim Ireland as their own. This first cycle featured the stories of the ancient gods, and his myth was one of its most famous.

The Woman Scorned

Midir the Proud, brother and foster father to Aengus, was once the king of the fairy people known as Tuatha De Danann. He and his wife Fuamnach lived together for many years, satisfied with their relationship. They lived in Bri Leith, or more specifically, in the Hollow Hills.

One day while Midir was hunting with his men, he came across the most beautiful young maiden he had ever seen washing her hair by the stream. He discovered that she went by the name of Etain. The pair instantly fell in love, and Midir wanted to wed her and bring her home to Bri Leith. She agreed to the marriage, and the two were wed shortly after.

Midir and Etain spent a lot of time together, and word of her beauty swept quickly throughout the kingdom. The two rarely parted, as Midir could not stand to be away from her for long. He neglected the needs of his first wife, which prompted a fury complete with magic and revenge. After seeing her husband in the arms of another, the comfort and love she once had darkened with rage, betrayal, and jealousy. In her misery, she recruited the help of a druid for a magical spell.

The druid Bressal, along with Fuamnach, entered the bedchamber of Etain at night while she slept. Bressal then conjured a storm and transformed Etain from the fairest maiden of the land to a fly. The tempest then swept her in its winds and cast her far away from the castle of her love, Midir the Proud.

The Life of a Fly

For seven long years, Etain was whipped around the country by the storm that left her wings battered and torn. Her seven years of endless flight met their end when she landed on the windowsill at Bru na Boinne. Finally able to rest, she climbed into the bedchambers of Aengus while he was present.

Aengus immediately recognized Etain as she was; he saw right through the spell that had been cast on her by the druid and Fuamnach. As much as he tried, he wasn't able to completely undo the spell. He was able to give her the closest thing to her human form as she could get. From dusk until dawn, Etain was returned to her human self. Aengus planted the most aromatic and colorful flowers and shrubbery in the sunniest corners of his garden for her personal use, as she spent her days as a fly.

Over time, Aengus and Etain grew closer and eventually fell in love. The couple believed that they would spend many long, happy years together. The only predictable thing about life is its unpredictability; soon the scorned first wife of Midir discovered her rival's place of refuge.

Fuamnach transformed into a raven and observed from an apple tree located in the center of the garden. She picked out the delicate Etain as she moved from flower to flower. In one swoop of her beak, Fuamnach snatched Etain and conjured another powerful storm. Yet again, she was swept away from her home, way past the fairy mounds and into a territory where few fairy-folk ever dared to go.

After the second disappearance of Etain, Aengus realized that she was kidnapped by the jealous Fuamnach. In his rage, he threw a magical potion into the air and called upon the gods to end her misery on earth. In the meantime, Etain was roped into another gust of wind, where she blew into the kingdom of Ulster.

The Ulster king Etar was holding a grand feast with his nobles, who were packed inside the castle for a night of dancing and merriment. Etar was sitting beside his wife, enjoying the festivities. She was cradling a goblet of wine in her hands as she enjoyed her time beside her husband.

Exhausted, Etain flopped onto the wine goblet's rim. Drawn by its sweet aroma, she leaned forward to take a small drink. She slipped and splashed into the wine as the queen moved the goblet to her mouth. The queen swallowed Etain. In the weeks that followed, Etar's wife discovered her miraculous pregnancy, carrying Etain to her next life as a mortal. The gods granted Aengus's cry for help as soon as Etain was swallowed and nestled inside the womb of a mortal queen. Etar and his wife welcomed a little girl named Etain. She was the same Etain as before, minus the memories of her previous life.

In the years before Midir and Etain were reunited, Aengus pursued his foster mother in a quest for revenge. He tracked her down to where she stayed with her druid friend Bressal and decapitated her. He carried his brutal trophy back home to the Bru na Boinne.

Together at Last

Midir and Etain were reunited many years later after she was already married to the king of Erin known as Eochu. Eochu also had a brother named Ailill, who grew gaunt with the sickness of his unrequited love for Etain. When her husband left the castle on a tour of his kingdom, Ailill confessed his love for her, and the only cure for his sickness was her. She wanted him to feel better, so she agreed to meet him in a cottage on the hill away from prying eyes and to keep the affair out of the king's bed.

Midir infiltrated the castle walls and disguised himself as Ailill each of the three times. She met with Midir, but she understood that something was off about her husband's brother. Instead of having relations with the imposter, she conversed with Midir. On the third meeting, Midir finally confessed who he was and the maiden she was before.

At first, she refused to believe that she was a born-again mortal. After much convincing, she eventually believed Midir and agreed to go back home with him only if Eochu allowed it. Upon Eochu's arrival back to his castle, Midir challenged him to a game of chess.

Eochu at first appeared to be the superior player. The stakes were constantly raised, with ever-increasing losses for Midir. In the very last game, Midir proposed a challenge where the winner was allowed to kiss and embrace Etain. Believing that he would win, Eochu agreed to the challenge. Unfortunately, the king lost the wager. A condition that he created was that Midir could claim his prize after a year.

During that year, Eochu demanded that his castle become heavily guarded in preparation for his foe's return. Despite the numerous guards, Midir slipped inside the castle undetected. There, he confronted the king to claim his prize. When the king agreed to allow the two to kiss and embrace, both Etain and Midir turned into swans and flew away.

Midir and his true love changed into swans in order to finally enjoy the life they had wanted together after years of waiting. In this next myth, there are some similarities between both brothers as they search endlessly for their true love.

The Dreams of Aengus

Being the god of love certainly had its perks, and Aengus often took advantage of it. He could make any woman fall in love with him, whether she was a mortal or even a powerful goddess. He used his good looks and velvety tongue to lure women into his bed. In addition, the birds that surrounded him sang beautiful songs, which aided him in his process of wooing women.

The Woman of His Dreams

Aengus dreamt of a beautiful maiden one night as he slept. Though he did not know her name, he instantly fell for her beauty alone. With a start, he awoke and realized that he had just seen the face of his true love. His heart twisted in longing and anguish over not being able to know her, so he recruited the help of his mother Boann and a cattle goddess by the name of Bealach na Bo Finne.

They searched the land for one year before returning exhausted and empty-handed. The goddesses could not find the mysterious woman from Aengus's dreams. Distraught, he asked his father, the Dagda, for help finding his lost love. Another year passed before the Dagda returned to reveal that he could not find the young maiden, either.

In a final attempt to find his long-lost love, Aengus asked one of the Dagda's friends, King Bodg Derg of the Munster kingdom, for aid. Again, Aengus waited a year before Bodg Derg returned, but this time revealed how he had found her at last. He gave her location to Aengus, then gave him her name: Caer Ibormeith.

Learning everything he needed to know, he set off to find the love of his life.

A Needle in a Haystack

Upon the arrival of Aengus to his lost love's location, it was the last day of Samhain or modern-day Halloween. On the shore of the lake known as Dragon Mouth, he discovered 150 women with chains binding them by pairs. He knew that his true love was here, waiting for him to free her from captivity.

Outraged, he started a conversation with the women's captors. It was then discovered that at the end of Samhain, all the women would be transformed into swans for one year. Aengus explained that he believed one woman was his soulmate. He wagered that if he could find his maiden as a swan, he would be allowed to marry her. The captors agreed to the bet. As he gazed upon the faces of these 150 women, he recognized the face of the woman in his dreams. Her eyes were filled with hope as his gaze landed on her and recognition flooded his face.

The Love of a Swan

After the women were transformed into swans, it seemed hopeless for Aengus. There was no way to determine Caer from any other swan based on their current physical appearance. He pondered for a brief moment before he also decided to find his love by turning himself into a swan. After his transformation, he called out to his true love, who then answered him back.

Aengus and Caer were finally united after many dreams about her. Once they discovered each other, the couple flew away while singing the most beautiful song known to man. Their harmony within the song cast a sleeping spell on her captors, which made them sleep for three full days before waking.

Since that night, the perfect pair transforms back into swans every other year at the end of Samhain. The couple, along with the other 149 women, all flock together and retain their swan form for the rest of the year. They remained in this eternal dance between forms with a never-ending love.

Conclusion

Aengus appeared in a total of five different myths in the Celtic pantheon. His influence and power within the context of the myths guaranteed his success as a god, and he was a beloved deity to the Celts. While the circumstances of his birth were scandalous, he was also a beacon of hope to the Celtic peoples. He and his brother Midir were able to find, and keep, the love they had been searching for, even through the painful waiting game. Aengus had many gifts, but the perseverance of love was his most notable.

Chapter 4: The Life of Lugh

As one of the most prominent gods of the Celtic pantheon, Lugh was a master of all crafts and believed in the value of oaths. He was unsurpassable in battle and was known as Lumfada or "long arm." This was in reference to the spear that he favored in battle and his mastery over the weapon. Both loved and feared, Lugh was, at one time, a ruler over the people of Tuatha de Danann. As the god of justice and oath keeping, it is probable that his name was a Celtic homage to the phrase meaning "to bind by oath." Despite being king and ruling over justice, he also used trickery to cheat, lie, and steal in order to overpower his enemies.

Due to Lugh's importance to the pantheon, the Celts even had a festival named after him. On August first, the Celts celebrated the life and death of Lugh, especially over his victory in Tir na nOg, which will be covered later in this chapter. The life of Lugh was a fascinating one, which continued even after his death.

The Birth of Lugh

Just like Aengus, Lugh was a child born out of a scandalous environment. Different myths stem from this unique birth, but one stands out from the rest. Some myths claimed that his father Cian and mother Ethniu were married to cement a union between the people of Tuatha De Danann and the Fomorians. According to this myth, the Tuatha De Danann were in the process of invading the Fomorians, and the marriage was a result of a final peace between the realms. However, a later version of the myth emerged, which recounts the prophecy of his birth.

A Prophetic Vision

Balor, one of the legendary creatures of the Celtic pantheon, was the king of the Fomorians, a race of demonic people who dwelled in the depths of seas and lakes. One day, a druid spoke of a prophecy about Balor: that he would be slain by his grandson. Taken aback, Balor raced back to his castle and ordered his daughter Ethniu to be locked into a tower called Tor Mor, or "great tower," on Tory Island in Ireland.

She was not to learn of the existence of men to prevent pregnancy, and therefore, the prophecy. Ethniu was very young at the time of her imprisonment. Balor was meticulous about who would take care of his daughter, so he entrusted only women to care for her. In total, twelve women in varying shifts took care of her every need as she grew into adulthood.

The Fateful Night

Meanwhile, outside of the Tor Mor, there was a famous cow who produced milk so well-received, it attracted even the likes of Balor. The cow was being looked after by Cian, the father of Lugh, for his brother who was away at the time. Cian was also one of the healers of the gods, holding a well-respected position in the pantheon.

Balor, in his greed, wanted the magical cow for himself. He offered to purchase the cow, but Cian refused the offer. Enraged, Balor transformed into a little red-haired mortal with freckles, spinning a tale of woe. He deceived Cian, and through his trickery, he was able to convince Cian to give him the cow.

Soon after, Cian realized he had been tricked. He had heard rumors of a woman trapped in a tower, who also happened to be the daughter of Balor. Seeking vengeance for the thievery, Cian visited with a magic fairy named Birog, who had agreed to help him. She conjured a magic spell that transported him to the top of the tower where Ethniu was imprisoned.

After climbing in through a window, Cian introduced himself and started to woo Ethniu. Soon after, he seduced her and climbed back through the window to retrieve the stolen cow. Hopeful that the seeds of his revenge were sown, he fled the area.

The Almost-Drowned Child

Lugh, along with his two other siblings, was conceived that night. As time went by, Balor realized that his daughter was indeed pregnant. After she gave birth to her triplets, her father snatched them from her arms, gathered them in a bundle of sheets, and then ordered a servant to drown them in the lake. The servant obliged. She was able to drown the first two triplets but dropped the third into the harbor. This third child was Lugh, who was then rescued by Birog.

When Birog realized who the child's father was, she returned Lugh to Cian. To further protect his son, Cian made the decision to foster his son to someone. Varying retellings of the myth include Cian's brother Gavida, the god of all smithery; the sea god Manannan mac Lir; and even the Queen of Bilrog, Tailtiu, as his foster parents. Since Lugh was hidden, the day of Balor's vengeance never came, but it further cemented the prophecy that was to unfold.

Lugh and the Tuatha De Danann

After his miraculous survival, Lugh grew up to be a fine young gentleman. Over time, he mastered all the trades and skills, to the point where he wanted to become a member of the Tuatha de Danann. As a protector of the gods, he realized he could possess a significant amount of power and command the respect of lesser peoples.

Rejection and Trickery

Lugh possessed a mastery of every trade that he and the gods deemed valuable. Skills in trades such as blacksmithing, swordsmanship, history, poetry, sorcery, and many others were considered to be the top priority when allowing someone to be a ruler over a certain craft. He entered the Hall of Nuada in the realm of Tara, or the palace of the gods.

He knocked at the doors to the palace and demanded an audience with the king to showcase his skills. Those who were worthy of the king's attention were granted access to serve the king with their gifts. Lugh proved time after time that he was worthy of a spot on the Tuatha De Danann. Each time he was received by the doorman, however, he was turned away based on the roles already having already been filled.

After the final rejection, he realized he could not achieve his goal with one skill alone. Curious and formulating a plan, he asked the doorman if the role of mastery of every skill was taken; the reply was no. As a result, Lugh found himself as the god with the title of "master of every skill." After his audience with the king, he was henceforth known as Chief Ollam, or "master of all skills."

Savior of the Gods

When Lugh finally gained access to the palace, he found that his people were oppressed by the Fomorians. They were in constant fear and subservience to the Fomorians, which caught Lugh by surprise. The Fomorians held a contest to see who was the most skilled in several tasks, such as throwing a flagstone and combat. Lugh opposed the champion Ogma and won every contest, as his new name and title suggested. He then played the harp as entertainment for the Fomorians and the court.

Nuada, the current king of the gods, approached Lugh based on his skills and wondered if this young man would be their salvation. Lugh was then introduced to battle strategies as the Tuatha De Danann started making preparations for war against the Fomorians. However, their preparations would not last, as the First Battle of Moytura developed.

During this conflict, the Tuatha De Danann and the Fomorians came to a stalemate. Nuada had lost his right hand, and in accordance with their customs, was forced to step down. In the Tuatha De Danann traditions, a king was to remain unblemished; because the king had lost his hand, he was no longer able to be the king. As a result, the next in line was Bres, who delayed the war. Bres was a half-blood, with one parent being a Fomorian.

The Second Battle of Moytura

In time, Bres ruled over the Tuatha De Danann and contributed to their slavery to the Fomorians. King Bres ruled for 27 years, forcing his kingdom to bow to the will of the Fomorians. The first battle of Moytura faded from everyone's mind, except for Lugh's. As King Bres reigned, Lugh set off to find and reclaim the throne for Nuada, the rightful king. Wright states that Lugh, along with two others who are claimed to be Cian's father and brother, helped to forge two fists: one constructed of silver, and the other of flesh, to return to Nuada to help him reclaim the throne. Once Nuada was whole again, Lugh was able to rally troops together and prepare for another war.

Before the final battle at Moytura, Lugh inspired the troops by asking what skills they brought. As he called upon each man and woman, their inspiration and determination to win the battle escalated. Many of the troops knew they would not be returning from the battle, but their will to fight for freedom from oppression and slavery outshined even the mighty spirits of gods and kings. After Lugh's final speech, they declared war against the Fomorians.

The Prophecy Unfolds

The brutal battle was long, bloody, and arduous. Blood was spilled by both sides as each fought valiantly. Exhaustion dripped from the limbs of all as the metal of opposing forces clashed. Heavy losses were incurred on both sides. Nuada dethroned Bres after gaining back his hand. After Bres's fall, the

Fomorians refused to accept their defeat; the Tuatha De Danann, inspired by the removal of a tyrant, fought harder.

Nuada was soon slain by Balor, after the dethroning of Bres. Balor decapitated the king in the middle of the battle. The sudden loss of their king impacted all the Tuatha De Danann. Many of them staggered once they realized what had happened to their king, but the sudden grief fueled their bloodlust and revenge. Lugh was no different and sought out his grandfather.

Before Balor was able to truly relish in his glorious kill, Lugh faced off against him. Recognition and fear radiated from the giant's one eye. He opened his other eye, notorious for poisoning all it gazed upon. Lugh was ready for this. Once the eye was opened, he loosed a stone from his trusted slingshot. The projectile hit Balor in the poisonous eye, killing him instantly. He toppled over, and the reign of terror died with him. The prophecy had come full circle.

Resolution

After the death of Balor, the tides changed in the favor of the Tuatha De Danann. Once the beloved king of the Fomorians fell, so did their will to fight. The Tuatha De Danann drove the Fomorians into the lake, which was then claimed as part of their realm. The battle was won, but there was one more loose end to be tied: how to handle Bres.

Lugh hunted Bres down after the battle was won, once Bres was alone, defenseless, and still on the battlefield. Bres begged on his hands and knees to be spared. Lugh obliged, but only if Bres agreed to share his knowledge of what and when to plant, sow, and reap the land of the Tuatha De Danann. Bres agreed to the conditions but was later killed by Lugh when he gave Bres the poisoned milk of 300 wooden cows and forced him to drink it.

Proving he was the master of all skills, especially of those in battle, Lugh was officially declared the king of the Tuatha De Danann. He ruled over the kingdom for many years—around 40—until his death and the beginning of the end of the Tuatha De Danann's reign.

The Death of the King

While praised for his ability to rule the kingdom of gods, Lugh was also a trickster and known for his constant affairs. Throughout his life, he had at least three different wives by the names of Bui, Buach, and Nas. It is currently unknown if his wives were all married to him at once, or if he divorced and remarried. Nevertheless, Lugh did not take well to his wives having extramarital affairs. One of his wives, Buach, had an affair with the Dagda's son Cermait.

Upon discovering the affair, Lugh killed Cermait in the fiery woes of revenge. Once his wife's lover was killed, he pretended as if nothing had happened and continued his life as usual. Cermait's three sons, Mac Cuill, Mac Greine, and Mac Cehct, began to plot their vengeance.

The sons of Cermait captured the once-great king and speared him through the foot, entrapping him on the bank of a lake. Afterward, they drowned him in the lake by forcing his head underwater until he could no longer breathe. He attempted to fight the three foes, but as his efforts grew weaker, the sons were able to overpower him. They left his body in the lake, giving it the name of Loch Lugborta.

After his mortal death, Lugh was sent to Tir na nOg, or the Overworld, the equivalent of Elysium and heaven in other pantheons and historical texts. The Overworld was also known as the land of endless youth, meaning that there was no death, sickness, or aging. Lugh often visited the mortal realm, and it was believed that after his death he sired the legendary Cu Cuthlainn.

Conclusion

The life and death of Lugh was a fascinating tale of deceit, revenge, and love all morphed into one. From the circumstances of his birth to his plot to become the king of the gods, Lugh was the child of prophecy and a god of justice. He was a deity not to be taken lightly in life or in death. The Celtic people drew wisdom and strength from his myths. A festival was exclusively made in his name to honor his life and journey to Tir na nOg. A favorite among the Celtic people, Lugh inspired all who honored him.

Chapter 5: The Dagda

The Dagda, also known as the superior king of the Celtic pantheon, was admired by the people for his jolliness and seriousness in equal measure. The Dagda was often portrayed as massive as a giant and with a tattered hooded cloak that was too small for him. Parts of his body were portrayed as larger-than-life. Because of Christianity's influence over the Celtic people, Catholics portrayed this deity as comical satire to undermine any authority that the deity had possessed.

The Dagda had many epithets and attributes, but he was most famous as the king of the gods. He ruled over the Tuatha De Danann for 80 years before his death, which allowed Lugh to rise from his reign. One of the most notable impacts on the Celtic pantheon was that it was a reminder that all things die, even the gods themselves.

The Dagda and the Magical Tools

The Dagda was notorious for having three magical tools in his possession as he ruled over the Tuatha De Danann: a magical cauldron, staff, and harp. Each represented his mastery in the particular field. These tools, along with how he was presented within the myths, showcased his brilliance and wisdom during his time as king.

The Cauldron

The cauldron he carried with him on journeys was rumored to be bottomless. Known as *coire ansic*, this magical bronze cauldron was known to never empty, giving everyone who ventured with him a full belly. It was also rumored that the ladle was so large, it could hold two men comfortably within it. The cauldron's magical abilities included resurrecting the dead and mending any type of injury.

This cauldron was also one of the Four Treasures of the Tuatha De Danann. Each treasure was located on a specific island complete with trials and a poet with a mastery over several arts: knowledge, Druidry, magical skill, and prophetic visions. In order to win one of these treasures, the challenger faced off against the poet to achieve full mastery of the subject.

There were four islands and cities associated with each of these skills. In the city of Falias was the poet Fessus, or Morfessa, who held the Stone of Fal. This treasure was associated with the king of Ireland as a whole, and therefore it imbued the king with powers. The city of Gorias with the poet Esras held onto a spear that Lugh later used in his life. The spear essentially gave the bearer invincibility against an army of foes. The city of Findias with the poet Uscias possessed the Sword of Light, which would later be given to Nuada. This rendered foes unable to escape from the sword once it was unsheathed. Finally, the cauldron was held by the poet Semias in the city of Murias.

Unfortunately, no story or myth exists currently about how the Dagda was able to land this cauldron in his possession. Scholars debate whether he earned the cauldron himself or took credit for another's work.

The Staff

Another of the Dagda's infamous keepsakes was the staff he always carried, called the *lorg mor*. In various translations of the myth, due to the Celts' many languages, the staff was also referred to as a club. In either case, this valuable weapon granted the Dagda's ability for both slaughter and resurrection.

There is only one myth that illustrated how the Dagda was lent the staff by three men carrying presents given to them by their father. This story began after the Dadga's son Cermait was killed by Lugh for having an affair with his wife. The Dagda found his son after Lugh had murdered him in revenge and carried Cermait on his back, weeping. He gently laid Cermait down on the ground after traveling a great distance and began uttering all the spells he knew to bring his son back from the dead. As he whispered various incantations, he also covered him in herbs.

It was all in vain. His son did not awaken, so the Dagda carried Cermait across the world until he was met with Eastern traders. He found three men, each carrying a gift their father had presented to them. The Dagda questioned what the gifts were, and they responded with three items: a cloak, a staff, and a shirt. The staff was imbued with magical powers of resurrection and destruction, the cloak allowed the wearer to shapeshift into anything while they were wearing it, and the shirt ensured the wearer would remain healthy from illness or sadness.

The Dagda was most interested in the staff. The three men described the powers of the staff to him. The smooth end was for resurrection, and the rough end had the ability to slay up to nine foes at once. He asked to borrow the staff and then proceeded to kill the men simultaneously. After the slaughter, the Dagda brought Cermait back to life. After Cermait reawakened, he convinced his father to also give the life back to the men he'd killed, and the Dagda agreed.

Once the men were alive, he allowed them to keep the cloak and the shirt so they would not be without them. The staff, on the other hand, was something he had initially borrowed and was not his to claim. The Dagda vowed that once it was time for him to die, the staff would return to its rightful owner.

The Harp

His trusted harp, also known as the *uaithne* or the "Four Angled Music," was also imbued with distinctive magical properties. The harp itself was composed of oak wood and ornamented with gold and jewels. As much of a magnificent sight as it was to behold, the music that the Dagda played was indescribable. It granted the Dagda the power to change the mood of anyone within earshot, as well as change the seasons.

While it is currently unknown how the harp came into the Dagda's possession, there is a myth that surrounds it. In the Second Battle of Moytura, the Dagda used the harp's magic to sway the opposing forces. In battle, he played musical chords to inspire men to forget their fears and focus on bloodlust and revenge. When the battle was finished, it allowed the men to remember the glory of battle instead of the pain of their injuries and sadness over lost brothers-in-arms.

Before the Second Battle of Moytura was won, the harp was stolen one night while the Fomorians and Tuatha De Danann were at war with each other. The Fomorians had heard of the Dagda's glorious harp and the power it provided. While the Dagda fought in the many battles, the Fomorians crept into his unguarded home to steal the harp. After their successful theft, they believed that the harp would benefit them while simultaneously weakening the Tuatha De Danann.

In response to his harp being stolen from him, the Dagda raced to the headquarters, an old, abandoned castle that the Fomorians were using as temporary shelter. The harp hung on a wall behind where all the Fomorians had gathered to eat and feast on their victory over their rivals. However, once the Dagda entered the abandoned castle, he called to his harp. The harp followed its master's voice until they were reunited. The Dagda played a song on the harp, prompting the women and children to cry; the men hid their faces in cloaks due to the shame they felt for stealing. The next song he played allowed all the Fomorians to laugh hysterically, to the point where they could not move. And finally, the last song he played was so peaceful that it lulled the population to sleep.

In the initial defense to stop the Dagda from reclaiming the harp, nine men lunged at him. With his staff, the Dagda killed the nine men all at once.

The Return of the Staff

The Dagda, along with the many deities including Lugh and Nuada, fought alongside each other in the Second Battle of Moytura against the Fomorians. In Celtic mythology, this battle was one of the remaining few left of the first mythological cycle called the Invasions Cycle, chronicling the rise and fall of the Tuatha De Danann. Within this battle, both sides incurred heavy losses, with the Dagda being one of them.

How to Woo the Goddess of War

Before the Second Battle of Moytura, the conflict between the Fomorians and the Tuatha De Danann was steadily becoming more intense. Each side knew that a battle would be inevitable; they'd already had a previous conflict, and once under the rule of Bres, the Fomorians became more arrogant and steadfast. However, the gods ensured that when the battle came, they would have a small edge over their opponents.

The Dagda was responsible for capturing livestock, including cattle and sheep, for milk and meat. He attempted to trick the Fomorians out of their important resources for feeding their armies with a focus on cattle and sheep. While his thievery did little overall, the result was to keep the Fomorians on their toes and aware of the Tuatha De Danann's presence.

As the tensions were reaching their climax, both sides prepared for war. The Dagda, in his infinite wisdom, paid the Morrigan, goddess of war, death, and prophecy, a visit. Being a king of gods had its perks, and the Dagda employed every privilege and prestige that came with the title. He visited the Morrigan while she bathed on Samhain, granting him access to her. She initially declined, knowing what the Dagda was truly after, but he seduced her anyway.

Impressed with his skill as a lover, she agreed to help the Tuatha De Danann by granting them her favor. Using her powers as a prophet, she granted him a vision of the imminent battle, in which the Tuatha De Dannan emerged victorious, but warned that there would be a heavy price to pay. Unconcerned, he left the Morrigan to continue working on battle strategies.

The Final Battle: Tuatha De Danann vs. Fomorians

During the Second Battle of Moytura, the Dagda implemented all three of his magical objects to aid him. As Lugh rallied the troops for battle, he called upon the Dagda, questioning what gifts he used to ensure the Tuatha De Danann won the battle. His mighty staff was the first he claimed, as it was able to kill nine enemies at once. He mentioned the harp as well, to frighten the Fomorians and bring a soundtrack to keep the soldiers filled with bloodlust and the glory of battle. The cauldron was to ensure that each man or woman would be fed and healed.

In the great battle, after Nuada fell at the hands of Balor, the Dagda rushed to aid his brother. Filled with rage and grief, he then launched himself into battle with the wife of Balor Cethlenn. As the two engaged in combat, she mortally wounded the Dagda with a projectile weapon such as a spear, but the weapon itself remains a mystery.

The battle was won, and the Tuatha de Danann emerged in victory as was prophesied. The Dagda returned to his home in Bru na Boinne, where he was laid to rest. His staff was then given back to the family of the three men from whom he had initially borrowed the item. As was promised by the Dagda himself, upon his death, the staff returned to its rightful owner.

The Dagda ruled over the Tuatha De Danann for 70-80 years, depending on the various retellings of the myth. Even though his physical body had died, his spirit continued to live.

As with most members of the Tuatha De Danann, when they die, they pass into the Overworld. Their spirit, however, can still be spoken to through fairy mounds. When one was in great need, they were able to call upon the god by speaking to his burial fairy mound located near his home.

Conclusion

The all-encompassing myths of the Dagda had spawned much speculation about the type of deity he was. He may not have been as notorious as other deities like Lugh or even the Morrigan, but the Dagda did have an exceptional arc for his development as a god and as a story itself. The Dagda was more known for his use of magical tools in battles, and of course, for siring the god of love Aengus by having an affair with the river goddess Boann. His many questionable choices led him down the path to many victories and success in his lineage as a deity. The Dagda was most likely the most powerful of all the kings of the gods, including Lugh. The next chapter will feature the infamous son of Lugh: Cu Chulainn.

Chapter 6: The Myths of Cu Chulainn

Perhaps one of the most widely known figures of the ancient Celtic pantheon, Cu Chulainn was considered a hero and an inspiration for many myths. From his birth to his death, Cu Chulainn was a figure who commanded respect and admiration from both his friends and enemies. The resulting myths of this figure still inspire this same fear and admiration to this day, as his stories are still passed down through the generations.

The Hound of Culann

Cu Chulainn's birth was the product of infidelity by the sun god Lugh himself. In some retellings of the myth, it was believed that Lugh impregnated a mortal woman by the name of Deichtine in a dream. Deichtine was married to Sualtam at the time. As much as it was believed that Cu Chulainn was a reincarnation of the sun god himself, the resulting pregnancy had Sualtam convinced his wife was having an affair. Soon after, the boy was born.

Setanta

It is currently a mystery how Sualtam reacted once he realized his wife had had an affair. No doubt there were questions about the birth of the child, but it seems as though Sualtam raised Cu Chulainn as if he were his own. Born with the name of Setanta, the young boy had a happy childhood. He was loved by his mother and stepfather, although they never told him of his true lineage. Setanta helped his family on their farm by milking cows, chopping wood, and doing other various tasks dedicated exclusively to a child.

Setanta was no ordinary child, however. He was obsessed with learning how to fight his opponents. One day when he was about five years old, he overheard some chatter among the local boys about a school dedicated to training the finest warriors in the land. The school was known as the Macra. If they passed the many examinations and showed promise in battle, the children would then be inducted into the famous guild for fighters known as the Red Branch Knights.

Setanta wanted to be a part of the action. He begged his parents to send him off to the school, but they informed him that he was still too young to go. After all, the cows weren't going to milk themselves.

Against his parents' wishes, he paid a visit to the school that very same day with a shield made of branches, a stick, and a hard ball. He trudged through the countryside until he came across the school. Children were playing a sport known as hurling, which is similar to field hockey in modern times. Being a talented player already, Setanta joined the game and quickly scored a goal.

The Foreshadowing of Greatness

The children were enraged at the new blood scoring a goal without a second thought. Setanta, confused by the sudden hostility, regained composure after the children started to throw their hurls and hard balls at him. A few hit him, but then he understood he was being attacked. Instead of turning and running, Setanta held his ground and dodged any punches thrown his way. In the end, he was surrounded by at least 30 children who were knocked out cold.

The school's headmaster and also the king of the area, named Conchobar, heard the commotion outside and headed outside of the castle walls to where he heard the clamor of fighting. Expecting to see something more catastrophic, he was pleasantly surprised when he saw Setanta encircled by the other children. The king automatically enrolled the young Setanta and even held a feast in his honor for that night at the castle.

The New Name

The king, occupied by having his friend Culann over for the feast, forgot about Setanta completely. Believing that everyone was accounted for, Culann allowed his dog to be unleashed as the guard to the entrance of the castle. The other students began to eat their meals; the king and his guest sat down to eat.

Setanta arrived at the king's castle to partake in the feast that was promised to him. Eager to begin his training, Setanta made his way to the castle walls when he was greeted by a hound guarding the entrance. The hound, not knowing that Setanta was a guest of the king, attacked. A fierce battle between the two forces erupted. Setanta dodged the attacks, and with one swift blow, he killed the hound in self-defense.

The screeches and growls attracted the king and Culann. The king remembered Setanta and rushed to aid him, fearing the worst for the child. Instead, he found the hound's broken body on the floor. Setanta was alive and for the most part unharmed, save for a few scratches from the tussle.

Culann wept over the loss of his guard dog. To make up for the misunderstanding, Setanta offered his services: he swore that he would guard Culann's home while a new dog was found and raised. Both the king and Culann were taken aback by a promise made by a child, but they also agreed to the arrangement.

Everyone in the banquet hall agreed that such a deed should not go unnoticed. A new name should be given to the boy who had killed such a mighty foe. From then onward, Setanta would be known as Cu Chulainn, or "the hound of Culann."

Other Retellings

While this retelling of the myth is catered more to children, there are variations of the myth that heighten the stakes. In one variation, the beginning is the same, but the conditions of the death of the hound are contrasting. In this version, Culann was not a friend of the king, but one of his enemies who tried to ambush and kill the king. Setanta arrived at the castle but instead was greeted with the sound of clanging metal. He rushed in to defend the king from the hound and killed it. Culann fled. However, the story of heroism still remains in the context of the myth.

The (Many) Lovers of Cu Chulainn

Cu Chulainn's prestige as a warrior followed him on his many journeys and battles over the years. As a young, attractive, and powerful man, he had his share of lovers. Infidelity ran rampant throughout the myths of the Celtic pantheon, and the story of Cu Chulainn was no different.

Young and Single

Many of the men with whom Cu Chulainn adventured were in constant worry that he would attempt to steal their wives. The young demigod was an attractive young man, and he would often use his looks to his advantage over women. To remedy this issue, the men looked far and wide for a suitable wife for Cu Chulainn, but to no avail. While many fell in love with him, he was not fond of them.

However, one woman caught the eye of Cu Chulainn. Her name was Emer, daughter of Forgall Monach, who was opposed to the match. He thought of a plan for Cu Chulainn to train over in Scotland with a warrior woman named Scathach. Her warrior skills were legendary, and he imagined that Cu Chulainn would be no match for her. When he suggested this to Cu Chulainn, he agreed and journeyed to Scotland to train. As he trained, he also fathered a son by the name of Connla but was not truly present in his life.

After his training, he returned to Ireland and demanded Emer's hand in marriage. Emer's father still did not approve of the marriage. Furious, Cu Chulainn stormed the castle walls and killed many of Monach's men, utilizing the training from Scotland with Scathach. Beaten, the king finally gave his blessing and allowed the two to marry.

The Death of His Son

Another myth involving this mighty warrior was the accidental death of his son Connla. The woman who bore his child was named Aife. She was Scathach's rival and, in some versions, her twin sister. Cu Chulainn and Aife engaged in battle, the two almost evenly matched, but Cu Chulainn had the upper hand. He tricked her, saying that in the thick of battle, her chariot and horses had fallen off a cliff. Aife's horses and chariot were her prized possession. With her distracted, he held a knife to her throat and demanded that she bear him a child.

After he left Scotland, Aife was still pregnant with his future son Connla. As the years passed, young Connla wanted to know who his father was. He ventured to Ireland in search of his father. In revenge for Cu Chulainn's absence, she told the young boy not to identify himself or back down from a fight. Connla was also trained in battle, so he believed that he would overcome any foe who opposed him. During the night, Connla arrived at the home of his father.

The noise of Connla's arrival alarmed Cu Chulainn. Grabbing his trusted spear, he hurled himself at the invader when he refused to identify himself. Believing that this was a threat, Cu Chulainn attacked Connla. Father and son engaged in a fierce battle, and Connla almost defeated Cu Cuthlainn. His father was quicker, and he hurled the spear at Connla, hitting him in the chest.

It was only after the berserk faded and the light of battle drained from his eyes that Cu Chulainn realized that he had killed his son.

The Jealousy of Emer

Emer knew of all Cu Chulainn's rendezvous with the ladies, and, while not an inherently jealous woman, she did get jealous if he fell in love with another. In this case, it was with Fand, the wife of the sea god Manannan mac Lir. Cu Chulainn rescued her from the Fomorians as they attacked the god on the seafront, which Manannan attended to, leaving her behind.

After the battle was won, Cu Chulainn and Fand saw each other and immediately fell in love. After he saved her, Cu Chulainn wanted her hand in marriage, and she agreed. Manannan knew the relationship was doomed from the start due to Cu Chulainn being mortal and Fand a fairy. He allowed the relationship to take its course.

On the other hand, however, Emer was not too thrilled to hear about this new marriage to another woman. In her rage, she attempted to kill the other woman, but Cu Chulainn was able to stop her before she killed Fand.

Fand was not upset by the potential assassination but was instead rather impressed at the amount of love Emer still had for her unfaithful husband. It was a love that was true, and Fand realized the two should be together after all. She then went back to her husband Manannan.

In order to ensure they would not remember their love for one another, Manannan waved his magical cloak in between them as a way for them to never meet again. Then they both drank elixirs to wipe away the memory of their love.

Conclusion

While the myths of Cu Chulainn were plenty, the main myths of his life and lovers are some of the most fascinating ones. Cu Chulainn was renowned for his skill in combat and the strategic wisdom he implemented throughout his time as a warrior. Born from a lineage of intense power, it was no wonder he was able to achieve near-impossible feats. The downfall of Cu Chulainn was not only the women he had attracted but the sons of the many enemies he had killed. As part of their reckoning, they weakened him through magic and finished him off. In his final moments, his life was cemented into the legends we know today. Despite being the most famous demigod of the Celtic pantheon, Cu Chulainn's popularity is rivaled by another legend which speaks of a child prodigy who grew up to be another hero the Celts praised.

Chapter 7: The Salmon of Knowledge

Finn mac Cumhail was one of the other heroes in the Celtic pantheon. He was a mortal, but his deeds over his lifetime granted him his legendary status. Similar to the rest of the stories in this book, his life was dramatic and filled with lust, betrayal, and battles over an heir. Nevertheless, the existence of Finn was one of the most celebrated myths throughout the pantheon. His wisdom and many victories in battle spawned numerous myths about him.

The Myth of Wisdom

The myth involving the Salmon of Knowledge began when Finn was a young boy. He was sent to become an apprentice for Finnegas, a widely recognized poet. O'Hara notes that the two often had adventures while reciting poetry, a celebrated art of the ancient Celts. Poetry was dedicated to recounting stories of the past, similar to the folktales we know today. The story of a salmon who was said to possess knowledge of the world emerged in conversation, and intrigued, Finn wanted to learn more. Finnegas recounted a tale of the salmon who had eaten a nut from the hazel tree of knowledge, and its traits were embedded into the salmon. It was believed that whoever ate the salmon would possess that same wisdom.

The River of Boyne

On a sunny morning during the spring, Finn and Finnegas stopped at River Boyne for a poetry session. As the two settled and discussed the story of the salmon, they placed their feet in the water and allowed the calm current to wash over them. Out of the corner of his eye, Finnegas believed he saw the glint of an eye under the water. He dove in and captured the fish, his eyes gleaming in triumph.

Finnegas believed that the salmon he held in his hand was the great Salmon of Knowledge. Finnegas asked the young apprentice to cook the salmon over a fire but did not fully trust his companion. He told Finn that he was forbidden to eat the fish. After all, he had waited many years to be blessed with the salmon. He craved the knowledge and wisdom the salmon was said to contain.

In the Flame

As the fish cooked, Finnegas left to grab extra supplies from his home, leaving Finn alone with the salmon. Finn grabbed a smooth stone from the surrounding riverbank and ignited a small fire. After several moments, the fish began to cook. The grease from the fish dripped into the flames, which caused Finn's stomach to growl. However, he refused to touch the fish at all costs.

After several minutes of cooking, it was time to flip it over to ensure an even cook. However, as he handled the fish, his thumb grazed the fish. Its juices scalded the young Finn, and the pain burned intensely. Without thinking, he jabbed the thumb into his mouth in order to dull the pain. It was then that he realized his mistake.

Finn, the Wisest of Men

As soon as Finnegas entered the campsite, he knew immediately something was wrong. The boy clutched his thumb in his hand with a haunted expression on his face. Finnegas demanded to know exactly what happened, and Finn explained the situation. With a deep sigh, Finnegas told the boy to eat the remainder of the salmon to see if it was imbued with wisdom.

In famished gulps, the boy devoured the fish, but nothing happened. There was no acute awareness, no sudden knowledge or understanding. Finnegas was relieved but also saddened that the fish was not the one of legend.

On a hunch and because of the pressure placed upon him by Finnegas, Finn put his thumb in his mouth again to see what would happen. At that moment, everything shifted. A spring of energy and understanding washed through him; the power of the salmon had finally taken its form. Head spinning from the rush of information, he sat down and explained the newfound knowledge that he gained.

From that moment forward, Finn was considered the wisest man in all the land. He was able to use this knowledge at will simply by biting his thumb. This wisdom aided him in the many battles that he would later face in his life, even up to his death. According to the ancient Celts, Finn was the embodiment of wisdom and courage.

Conclusion

The Celtic pantheon's core themes reflected mortality, love/lust, and the importance of defending loved ones. The druids, along with warriors, held responsibilities in equal measure: one tasked with the survival of cultural norms and religion, the other with the survival of their people as a whole. Memories of these times past have lived on in myth, but many other memories and traditions have been forgotten in time.

What remains of this unique and intriguing mythology still grants it immortality. It still continues to inspire creatives, no matter the medium, to create worlds and stories that will be forever embedded in the memories of those who experience them.

The myths and legends conveyed in this book, as well as the ones not mentioned here, remind us all that death is a natural cycle of life; no one is immune to it, not even the great gods of the Celtic pantheon. Even when we die, the stories of our lives will keep us immortal.

References

Badnjarevic, D. (2022, May 26). *A guide to 31 of the scariest Celtic and Irish mythological creatures*. The Irish Road Trip. https://www.theirishroadtrip.com/irish-mythological-creatures/

Bergin, O. (1927). *How the Dagda got his magic staff*. In Medieval Studies in Memory of Gertrude Schoepperle Loomis (pp. 789–790). Columbia University Press. https://maryjones.us/ctexts/dagda.html

Blevins, M. L. (2010, April 28). *The complete list of prominent Celtic gods and goddesses*. Historyplex. https://historyplex.com/celtic-gods-goddesses

Celtic gods & goddesses: The most important deities guide. (2022, May 9). Let's Go Ireland. https://www.letsgoireland.com/celtic-gods-and-celtic-goddesses/

Celtic Life International. (2020, October 26). *Top 10 Celtic monsters!* https://celticlifeintl.com/top-10-celtic-monsters/

Celtic Mythology. (n.d.). Myths and Legends. Retrieved October 27, 2022, from http://www.mythencyclopedia.com/Ca-Cr/Celtic-Mythology.html

Celtic mythology—Gods, symbols, myths and legends. (2018, June 18). The Mystica. https://www.themystica.com/celtic-mythology/

The Celtic religion. (n.d.). englishmonarchs.co.uk. Retrieved October 18, 2022, from https://englishmonarchs.co.uk/celts_21.html

Connor. (2020, February 15). *Dagda's harp and the Tuatha dé Danaan*. The Irish Place. https://www.theirishplace.com/heritage/irish-myths-and-legends/dagdas-harp-and-the-tuatha-de-danaan/

Derrig, J. (2022, June 25). *A guide to 12 infamous Celtic gods and goddesses*. The Irish Jewelry Company. https://www.theirishjewelrycompany.com/blog/post/a-guide-to-12-infamous-celtic-gods-and-goddesses

Dillon, M. & Mac Cana, P. (n.d.). *Celtic religion—Beliefs, practices, and institutions*. Britannica. Retrieved October 20, 2022, from https://www.britannica.com/topic/Celtic-religion/Beliefs-practices-and-institutions

Enya Quote. (n.d.). A-Z Quotes. Retrieved October 17, 2022, from https://www.azquotes.com/quote/1118583

Flores, P. (2018, March 29). *The scariest monsters and demons from Celtic mythology*. Core Spirit. https://corespirit.com/articles/the-scariest-monsters-and-demons-from-celtic-mythology

Gill, N. S. (2019, July 30). *A list of Celtic gods and goddesses*. ThoughtCo. https://www.thoughtco.com/celtic-gods-and-goddesses-117625

History.com editors. (2019, October 24). *Who were Celts*. HISTORY. https://www.history.com/topics/ancient-history/celts

Irish Central Staff. (2022a, October 27). *Scariest monsters and demons from Celtic myth for Halloween.* Irish Central Studio LLC. http://www.irishcentral.com/roots/history/monsters-demons-celtic-myth

Irish Central Staff. (2022b, October 28). *Top gods and goddesses from Celtic mythology.* Irish Central Studio LLC. http://www.irishcentral.com/roots/history/irish-centrals-top-ten-gods-and-goddesses-from-celtic-mythology-133143343-237789201.html

Jarus, O. (2014, April 7). *History of the Celts.* Future US, Inc. https://www.livescience.com/44666-history-of-the-celts.html

Javed, A. (2022, October 20). *Where did the Celts live/characteristics/religion/organization.* EngloPedia. https://englopedia.com/where-did-the-celts-live/

Kelly, D. (2022, February 17). *The untold truth of fallen angels.* Grunge. https://www.grunge.com/159512/the-untold-truth-of-fallen-angels/

Mala, A. (2021, July 13). *Danube river.* WorldAtlas. https://www.worldatlas.com/rivers/danube-river.html

O'Hara, K. (2022a, May 26). *Cu Chulainn: 8 mighty myths and legends I loved as a kid.* The Irish Road Trip. https://www.theirishroadtrip.com/cu-chulainn/

O'Hara, K. (2022b, May 26). *Fionn mac Cumhaill and the legend of the salmon of knowledge.* The Irish Road Trip. https://www.theirishroadtrip.com/the-salmon-of-knowledge/

O'Hara, K. (2022c, May 26). *The legend of the mighty Fionn mac Cumhaill (includes stories)*. The Irish Road Trip. https://www.theirishroadtrip.com/fionn-mac-cumhaill/

Rhys, D. (2021, April 29). *Legendary creatures of Celtic mythology – A list*. Symbol Sage. https://symbolsage.com/creatures-of-celtic-mythology/

Roberts, A. (2015, October 4). *The Celts: Not quite the barbarians history would have us believe*. Guardian News & Media Limited. https://www.theguardian.com/science/2015/oct/04/celts-great-torque-snettisham-hoard-british-museum-alice-roberts

Smit, J. L. (2020, April 20). *Celtic gods and goddesses: Exploring the pantheon and mythology of the ancient Celts*. History Cooperative. https://historycooperative.org/celtic-gods-and-goddesses-celtic-pantheon/

Sutherland, A. (2018, April 7). *Four magical treasures of Tuatha De Danann*. Ancient Pages. https://www.ancientpages.com/2018/04/07/four-magical-treasures-of-tuatha-de-danann/

Thalia. (2018, October 9). *The Dagda's cauldron*. The First Age. Retrieved October 29, 2022, from https://thefirstage.org/wiki/the-dagdas-cauldron/

The wooing of Etain. (n.d.). Emerald Isle. Retrieved November 13, 2022, from https://emeraldisle.ie/the-wooing-of-etain

Williams, A. (2021, December 23). *Morrigan*. Mythopedia. https://mythopedia.com/topics/morrigan

Winters, R. (2016, July 30). *Lugh of the long-arm: The martial and sovereign reach of Lugh Lama-fada.* Ancient Origins. https://www.ancient-origins.net/myths-legends/lugh-long-arm-martial-and-sovereign-reach-lugh-lama-fada-006367

Winters, R. (2019, 22 March). *The wooing of Etain: An Irish tale of love, loss, and jealousy.* Ancient Origins. Retrieved November 13, 2022, from https://www.ancient-origins.net/myths-legends-europe/wooing-etain-irish-tale-love-loss-and-jealousy-003077

Wright, G. (2021a, November 18). *Aengus.* Mythopedia.https://mythopedia.com/topics/aengus

Wright, G. (2021b, November 18). *Lugh.* Mythopedia. https://mythopedia.com/topics/lugh

Wright, G. (2021c, August 26). *Taranis.* Mythopedia. https://mythopedia.com/topics/taranis

Wright, G. (2022, November 2). *Dagda.* Mythopedia. https://mythopedia.com/topics/dagda

Zhelyazkov, Y. (2021, May 11). *Celtic mythology – An overview of a unique mythology.* Symbol Sage. https://symbolsage.com/celtic-mythology-overview/

www.ingramcontent.com/pod-product-compliance
Lightning Source LLC
Chambersburg PA
CBHW070938120626
46546CB00004B/1456

WHAT'S NEXT?

EONARD RESTALL, Ph.D

WORKBOOK PRESS LLC
187 E Warm Springs Rd,
Suite B285, Las Vegas, NV 89119, USA

Website: https://workbookpress.com/
Hotline: 1-888-818-4856
Email: admin@workbookpress.com

Ordering Information:
Quantity sales. Special discounts are available on quantity purchases by corporations, associations, and others.
For details, contact the publisher at the address above.

Library of Congress Control Number:

ISBN-13:   000-0-000000-00-0 (Paperback Version)
             000-0-000000-00-0 (Digital Version)

REV. DATE: 31/05/2022

What's Next?

Leonard Restall, PhD

CONTENTS

Acknowledgements

The completion of this book has been made possible by the encouragement of many people, including my late wife, Rita, and from research done by others which have been acknowledged throughout this book.

The inspiration to write this book as a companion to my previous one, *In Pursuit of Success: Overcoming Underachievement*, came about from a challenge made to me by a reporter. He was so surprised at my achievements: gaining a PhD at seventy years of age and publishing my first book at eighty-seven years. He said to me, 'What's next?' as if it would be natural for me to go on further.

I then considered some answers to the question, for it is unlikely that one could stop where one is and not lose ground as knowledge increases at such a fast rate. This same quandary could apply to anyone, but where does one start? This book endeavours to show ways to answer this dilemma and gain further success.

I acknowledge the knowledge and inspiration gained from Professor John Malone of Curtin University, Perth, Western Australia, and Professors Alan Webster, James Chapman, and Don McAlpine from Massey University, New Zealand. Wishing you much success as you answer your own question: what's next?

Notes

Characteristics of Individual Types
What Are You Like?

Now that you have found out your type and also the characteristics of your type, the next stage is to find out something about your attitude and the way you think, which will help you in deciding what's next. You may find that you do not always think or act like someone else because you may have a different personality or individuality. This is one of the advantages of finding out your 'type'.

There are sixteen individual types contained within the Myers-Briggs type inventory, and these are given in this section together with some of the distinguishing characteristics found in the sixteen types.[3] You may find that even with two people of identical type, there may be slight differences, which do not affect the type description but may show out in slight differences in characteristics between individuals.

For example, there are two people with the same type description but with differences in scores shown within the four scales. They may be identified as being the same type but not quite the same in personality characteristics.[1,3]

Consider the case of one person scoring 3 for introvert and 2 for extrovert, indicating an introvert type. Another person with 4 for introvert and 1 for extrovert would also be identified as an introvert type, but the slight difference in strength within this dimension could be a reason for differences. The first of these two persons will generally show out less for introversion characteristics than the second but still tend towards introversion.[3]

This example has only considered one of the four scales, so with the many variations possible within the scales, differences can be expected. However, there will be many other characteristics that will be similar for these two persons.[3] Now here are the sixteen types.[1,3]

ESFJ. This type tends to be energised or are interested by what goes on in their outer world and may be more inclined to make decisions based upon their feelings and emotions towards people or towards action rather than ideas.

They relate well to people and may like to have people around them in the working environment, such as the classroom. They are able to block out noise while they work and like to get things settled and finished. They often show a liking for talking and sharing with others and may prefer to learn new tasks by talking it through with someone else and then working alone. They enjoy learning new skills and dislike doing the same things repeatedly. They tend to have good achievement motivation.

The communication preference for this type tends to be by talking rather than writing. They give most attention to facts that come from practical experience and are realistic and practical.

The following occupations would be very suitable for this type and have a high probability for success: advertising officer, guidance counsellor, public relations officer, radio/TV personality, real estate agent, receptionist, personnel manager, social worker, and travel agent.[1,3]

ESFP. This type tends to be energised more by what goes on in their outer world of people or action and may be inclined to be outwards-looking rather than looking towards ideas. They may study with background musicians. They generally enjoy learning new skills and dislike doing the same things repeatedly.

They may prefer to learn new tasks by talking them through with others and may enjoy practical tasks better than theory. They communicate better by talking than by writing and enjoy the opportunity to talk.

They may remember things best when they are seen or read and seem to be able to study well with a background music.

They can work on one project for a long time and consider themselves responsible for their own learning. They adapt well to changing situations and may prefer a flexible, spontaneous way of doing things better than a planned, orderly, and decided way.

Decisions will be strongly based on knowing all the facts about a new job or task, but they may have trouble making decisions, feeling they never have enough information.

The following occupations would be very suitable of this type and have a high probability for success: occupational therapist, personnel manager, public relations officer, psychologist, radio/TV personality, real estate agent, receptionist, advertising officer, auctioneer, and guidance counsellor.[1,3]

ESTJ. This type tends to be energised more by what goes on around them. They may be inclined to be outward-looking towards the world of people and action rather than with ideas. They may choose to have people around them in their working environment, such as the classroom, and prefer to learn a new task by talking it through with someone else. They possibly are better working in pairs rather than with a group. They may find that they like to move around within the classroom.

They tend to work better in the morning than in afternoons and may be easily motivated. They enjoy learning new skills and generally consider themselves responsible for their learning and like to get things settled and finished. They may like structured and organised learning tasks better than random events and work better when they can plan and follow their own plan.

They show a preference for a planned, systematic, orderly way of life better than a flexible, spontaneous way. They tend to have good achievement motivation.

Their communicative preferences tend to be by talking rather than writing, and they give most attention to facts that come from personal experiences. This makes them practical and realistic. They would rather work with known facts than look for possibilities and relationships.

Their judgements are based more on impersonal analysis and logic than on personal values. They may be inclined to follow their own inspiration or hunches. They may enjoy work where their results are immediate, clear, and tangible.

The following occupations would be very suitable for this type and have a high probability for success: store manager, travel agent, writer, lawyer, market researcher, personnel manager, planner, public relations officer, salesperson, school administrator, and shop owner.[1,3]

ESTP. This type tends to be energised more by what goes on around them. They may be inclined to be outwards-looking towards the world of people and action rather than with ideas. They may choose to have people around them in their working environment, such as the classroom, and prefer to learn a new task by talking it through with someone else. They can study with background music and generally enjoy learning new skills. They dislike doing the same things repeatedly.

They may like being flexible and spontaneous in doing things rather than having a planned, orderly way. Their judgements are more than likely based on impersonal analysis and logic than on personal values. They usually reach a conclusion step by step and are careful about facts. They can likely gain better results if they plan their work schedules.

The following occupations would be very suitable for this type and have a high probability for success: interior decorator, landscaper, librarian, mechanic, secretary, accountant, architect, bank teller, bookkeeper, caretaker, bus driver, designer, electrician, forest ranger, cook/chef, and receptionist.[1,3]

ENTJ. This probably relates more to the outer world of people and things than to the inner world of ideas. They may feel energised by what goes on in the world outside of them than on their inner feelings.

They likely prefer to work on their own, and they show a preference to their inspiration or inches and enjoy learning new skills. They can block out noise or sound when they work. They may tend to make quick decisions.

It is likely that they give most of their attention to facts that come from practical experience and have a practical use. They are usually good at anything that requires reasoning and intelligent talk. They may learn better in the afternoon.

They may prefer a planned, decided, orderly way of life better than a flexible, spontaneous way.

The following occupations would be very suitable for this type and show a high probability for success: administrator, chemist, biologist, curator, engineer, journalist, librarian, market researcher, psychologist, reporter, school administrator, and public relations officer.[1,3]

ENTP. This type tends to be energised or is interested by what goes on in their outer world and may be more inclined to make decisions based on outside events rather than their inner feelings, although they are inclined to make decisions on their intuitive perception of things rather than knowing all the facts.

It is likely they prefer to have people around them in their working environment, such as the classroom, and may prefer to learn new tasks by talking them through with others. They generally enjoy learning new skills. They may like to be free to move around the classroom during learning activities.

They probably would rather look for possibilities and relationships than work with known facts. They may be resourceful in solving new and challenging problems but may neglect routine assignments. They are likely skilful in finding logical reasons for what they want. Also, they may feel they know about things without checking out all the details.

They prefer a flexible, spontaneous way of life better than a planned, decided, and orderly way.

The following occupations would be very suitable for this type and show a high probability for success: personnel manager, occupational therapist, public relations office, psychologist, radio/TV personality, real estate agent, receptionist, advertising officer, and guidance counsellor.[1,3]

ENFJ. This type probably relates more easily to the outer world of people and things than to the inner world of ideas. They may feel energised by what goes on in the world outside of them and their feelings than on their inner world of ideas. Activities involving understanding and communication with people could be very suitable for this type.

They likely prefer to learn a new task by talking it through with someone else or working within a group. They do like learning activities that require diagrams or illustrations. They dislike doing the same things repeatedly and like to be free to move around the classroom during learning activities.

They tend to be enthusiastic and insightful and usually look for possibilities and relationships rather than problems and may feel that they know about things without checking out all the details. Their judgement tends to be based on personal values than on impersonal analysis and logic. They consider themselves responsible for their learning. They tend to prefer the adult company to that of their peers.

The following occupations would be very suitable for this type and have a high probability for success: advertising officer, guidance counsellor, occupational therapist, personnel manager, psychologist, public relations officer, radio/TV personality, real estate agent, and receptionist.[1,3]

ENFP. This type probably relates more easily to the outer world of people and things than the inner world of ideas They may feel energised by what goes on in the world outside of them and their feelings than to their inner world of ideas. Activities involving understanding and communication with people could be very suitable for this type.

They would rather look for possibilities and relationships than work with known facts and tend to make judgements based on personal values than on impersonal analysis and logic. They may be quick with a solution for any difficultly and are ready to help with such a problem.

They may like to have people around their working environment, such as the classroom, and like to be free to move around the classroom. They like to learn new tasks by talking them through with others and like activities that require the use of diagrams. They tend to prefer the adult company to that of their peers.

They probably prefer a flexible, spontaneous way of life better than a planned, decided way. Often, they rely on their ability to improvise instead of preparing in advance.

The following occupations would be very suitable for this type and show a high probability for success: advertising officer, guidance counsellor, occupational therapist, personnel manager, psychologist, public relations officer, radio/TV personality, real estate agent, and receptionist.[13]

ISTJ. This type tends to relate more easily to their inner world of ideas than to the outer world of people and things. They tend to base their judgements more on impersonal analysis and logic than on personal values.

They are inclined to be serious and thorough in all their attempts and work steadily towards what they have set their mind on. They tend to have good achievement motivation.

They refer quietness for concentration and can work on projects for a long time without interruption but dislike doing the same thing repeatedly. They consider themselves responsible for their learning and prefer working on their own. They tend to be matter-of-fact, realistic, and dependable and prefer practical tasks when learning rather than theory. They prefer an adult company to that of their peers.

They prefer a planned, decided, orderly way of life better than a flexible, spontaneous way.

The following occupations would be very suitable for this type and show a high probability for success: administrator, biologist, botanist, chemist, computer programmer, conservationist, doctor, journalist, laboratory technician, librarian, market researcher, medical technologist, nutritionist, optometrist, pharmacist, professor, proofreader, psychologist, reporter, researcher, scientist, teacher, and writer.[1,3]

ISTP. This type tends to relate more easily to their inner world of ideas than to the outer world of people and things. They tend to be quiet and reserved and analytically observe life. They tend to base their judgements more on impersonal analysis and logic than on personal values.

They may prefer to work alone on problems and have a routine or established way of doing things but may require time to complete tasks and like to get things settled and finished. They tend to work with bursts of energy powered by slack periods in between and may exert themselves no more than necessary because of their efficient ways of working.

They can adapt to changing situations but require having all the facts before making a decision; they may display a preference for practical tasks when learning rather than theory. Usually, they may find themselves interested in impersonal matters, cause and effect, and mechanical things. They may have problems relating to achievement motivation.

They prefer a flexible, spontaneous way of life better than a planned, orderly way.

The following occupations would be very suitable for this type and show a high probability for success: accountant, agriculture, architect, auditor, boatbuilder, bookkeeper, builder, bus driver, caretaker, cook/chef, computer programmer, computer operator, designer, electrician, farmer, fireman, fashion designer, flight attendant, forest ranger, surveyor, tailor, truck driver, waiter, woodworker, and X-ray technician.[1,3]

ISFJ. This type tends to relate more easily to their inner world of ideas than to the outer world of people and things. They may be more energised by what goes on within their thoughts than the world outside. They tend to be patient with detail and routine things.

They may prefer to work with known facts than to look for possibilities and are careful to use all the facts before making decisions.

Generally, they tend to be thorough, painstaking, and accurate but require plenty of time to complete tasks. They make themselves responsible for their learning and like quietness for concentration and can work with 'bursts' of energy powered by the enthusiasm with slack periods in between. They prefer practical tasks and learning rather than theory and like to get things settled and finished. They like learning activities that require diagrams and illustrations.

They probably make their judgements based on personal values and the effect they may have on others. They likely prefer a planned, orderly way of life better than a flexible, spontaneous way.

The following occupations would be very suitable for this type and show a high probability for success: accountant, agriculture, architect, bank teller, boatbuilder, bookkeeper, bus driver, caretaker, cook/chef, computer programmer, computer operator, designer, electrician, farmer, fireman, fisherman, flight attendant, interior decorator, landscaper, mechanic, metalworker, office worker, plumber, postman, receptionist, secretary, statistician, surveyor, tailor, waiter, welder, woodworker, and X-ray technician.[1,3]

ISFP. This type tends to relate more easily to their inner world of ideas than to the outer world of people and things. They may feel more energised by what goes on within their thoughts than on the world outside. They tend to work alone on problems rather than in a group and tend to be patient with detail and routine things but require plenty of time to complete tasks and learn new things.

They like quietness for concentration and consider themselves responsible for their learning. They can adjust well in changing situations. They may dislike doing the same things repeatedly and tend to make decisions quickly and may be quick and spontaneous in solving problems.

They probably make the decisions based on personal values and the effect they may have on others. They generally dislike disagreements and do not like to force their opinion on to others. They are often relaxed about getting things done and may not be concerned with time.

They are likely to prefer a flexible, spontaneous way of life better than a planned, decided way.

The following occupations would be very suitable for this type and show a high probability for success: artist, commercial artist, conservationist, fashion designer, florist, waiter, zoologist, and childcare provider.[1,3]

INTJ This type tends to relate more easily to their inner world of ideas than to the outer world of people and things. They tend to work alone on problems rather than in groups but may require time to complete tasks. They enjoy learning new skills. They generally like quietness for concentration. The layout of the classroom can be important to this type.

They tend to work in bursts of energy powered by the enthusiasm with slack periods in between. They dislike doing the same things repeatedly and like to get things settled and finished but may look for novel ways of solving problems.

They may tend to be sceptical, critical, independent, determined, and stubborn in order to complete tasks they start on.

They probably prefer to base their judgement on impersonal analysis and logic than on personal values. It is likely that they like a planned, decided, orderly way of life better than a flexible, spontaneous way and have a great drive for their ideas.

The following occupations would be very suitable for this type and show high probability for success: lawyer, market researcher, marketing officer, personnel manager, pilot, plumber, police officer, politician, professor, public relations officer, reporter, salesman, school administrator, shop owner, store manager, and travel agent.[1,3]

INFP. This type tends to relate more easily to their inner world of ideas than to the outer world of people and things. They may prefer to work alone on problems but may require time to complete tasks. They would rather work with possibilities and relationships than work with known facts.

The layout of the classroom is important for this type. They enjoy learning new tasks but dislike doing the same thing repeatedly. They may find that they get absorbed with their work and may be inclined to do too much. They can adapt well to changing situations and tend to best remember things that are seen or read.

They tend to base their judgement more on personal values than on impersonal analysis and logic, and it is likely they prefer a flexible, spontaneous way of life better than a planned, orderly way.

The following occupations would be very suitable for this type and show a high probability for success: administrator, botanist, chemist, computer programmer, curator, doctor, engineer, laboratory technician, nutritionist, optometrist, pharmacist, professor, proofreader, psychologist, reporter, researcher, school administrator, scientist, teacher, and writer.[1,3]

Supplementary Notes Regarding Individual Type Profiles

The following gives some of the strong points associated with the sixteen individual types. Some of these points may show out more than others.

ESFJ
Gregarious—Supportive—Sympathetic—Cooperative—
Popular—Respects tradition—Gracious—
Personable—Conscientious—Helps friends

ESFP
Open and outgoing—Pleasant—Cooperative—
Positive and upbeat—Empathetic—People-oriented—
Tolerant—Realistic—Quick to act—Adaptable

ESTJ
Deals in reality—Goal-oriented—Responsible—
Stable—Systematic—Conscientious—Organiser—
Thorough—Decisive—Logical and objective

ESTP
Easy-going—Prepared for action—Lively and
quick—Realist—Resourceful—Spontaneous—
Versatile—Entertaining—Persuasive—Alert

ENFJ
Loyal—Diplomatic—Harmonious—People-oriented—Expressive—
Responsible—Idealist—Supportive—Communicative—Concerned

ENFP
Charismatic—Has a zest for life—Discerning—
Dynamic—Impromptu—Energetic and enthusiastic—
Intuitive with people—Versatile—Imaginative

ENTJ
Gregarious—Quick-witted—Controlled objectivity—Firm yet fair—
Efficient—Logical—Verbalises easily—Seeks challenge—Strategic

ENTP
Understands people—Enjoys new projects—Open-
minded—Communicative—Curious and interested—
Likes variety and action—Instinctive—Analytical—
Enjoys a challenge—Enthusiastic and energetic

ISFJ
Sympathetic—Detailed and factual—Conscientious—
Respects tradition—Sense of history—Impromptu—
Down to earth—Sense of justice—Service-oriented—
Meticulous with detail—Practical and organised

ISFP

Gentle and considerate—Quiet disposition—Has an
inner intensity—Can act spontaneously—Is in touch
with reality—Unpretentious—Sensitive to others—
Artistic—Unassuming—Cooperative and balanced

ISTJ

Thorough—Factual—Tangible—Consistent—Committed—
Reliable—Reserved—Orderly—Systematic—Down to earth

ISTP

Reserved—Factual—Logical—Adaptable—Independent—
Practical—Down to earth—Analytical—Prudent—Spontaneous

INFP

Idealist—Supporter of causes—Faithful—Searches
for the truth—Noble—Honourable—Harmonious—
Dedicated to duty—Gentle/polite—Committed

INFJ

Considerate—Highly committed—Calm and
sensitive—Harmonious—Warm—Inspires others—
Compassionate—Reserved—Accepts challenges

INTJ

Highly practical—Systematic—Individualistic—Mentally
quick—Committed—Detached—Independent—
Determined—Visionary—Self-motivated—Logical

INTP

Original—Future-oriented—Inquisitive—
Speculative—Reserved—Global thought—Analytical—
Independent—Determined—Uses abstract ideas

Introduction

What's Next?

- an expression of surprise, wonder, doubt, or anticipation
- a question to you or from you
- a personal desire to advance or change ideas.

This book has been written to follow as a companion to *In Pursuit of Success: Overcoming Underachievement.*

It came about after a newspaper reporter was amazed by my history of finishing a PhD at the age of seventy and publishing my first book at the age of eighty-seven. He then asked, 'What's next?' So this gave me a good reason to pursue this expression, which can be one of surprise, doubt, anticipation, and question or one of continuing on the road to further success.

It may be an expression made by someone other than you or to you or one you make yourself. It may be in the form of a question or a challenge as to what you can do next or where to go next. In answering such a question, the amount of interest shown will be a strong motivator for you.

If there is no positive answer to the question or statement, it is unlikely that you will take it further. I have found that if there is no ongoing attempt to advance and just deciding to stay where one is, it is likely to cause one to slip back because knowledge has a very short half-life. This is very likely for a person who has gained much but is satisfied with his or her success.

There are many examples of people gaining more than one PhD, as was the case of Albert Einstein. This writer was tempted to do something similar and advance knowledge further by trying for a second PhD. The reason is that once you have found out so much *new* knowledge, it very often reveals what is still lacking that may be advanced beyond where one is at.

This book gives positive steps to advance from any expression of 'What's next?' and enables you to find yourself achieving great success. Avoid the tendency to stay where you are but go where you would like to be.

A good starting point can be in the area of your occupation: are you in the best one for your individuality? It is estimated that about 80 per cent of people are in occupations unsuited to their individuality and don't realise it other than the fact that they may not be enjoying the one they are in. So is this your 'What's next?'

Here is a very good strategy to help you to deal with what's next:

- Look outward—at what is involved.
- Look inward—to what gifts you have.
- Look upward—for inspiration.
- Look forward—to what results you are expecting.

So now you may be equipped with the answer to what's next and have gained greater fulfilment of life and satisfaction. Learning can be much fun and enjoyable. You now may be ready to get started to answering what's next and make great headway towards further success.

Chapter 1

As a man thinks, so is he.
Proverbs 23:7

In order to change one's lifestyle, it is vital that one changes their thinking. Thinking occurs in the mind and is necessary to cause changes to affect one's actions. Just how to change one's thinking will be covered in more detail later, but keep in mind that it can have a great effect upon your response to the question posed in the title of this book.

The question, command, prediction, or prophecy 'what's next?' can be either or all and can have a tremendous effect on your destiny, but it depends upon what you do with it. It may depend upon whether you ask the question of yourself or whether someone asks the question for you.

In many cases, people may not be aware of what is likely to happen next or may not be thinking about the possibilities of being able to influence what will be next for them. But this book will provide ideas to cause you to determine what you would like to happen next so as to avoid random consequences or even no further planned happenings occurring in your life. Why not pursue a positive direction for your life by making positive choices and developing goals for your life? This is what I had decided, and you may read about one of the positive consequences for me.

Having completed my PhD at the age of seventy and then published my first book at the age of eighty-seven, I was asked by a news reporter, 'What's next?' This is a question that may be the name for the next TV program, but it could be an indicator of where you are or where you may be wanting to proceed to in life or what is it that you may be wanting to do, such as develop a new project or invention. It basically is a question as to what you are wanting to do or be. Without it, you may be wandering around quite aimlessly or randomly expecting the good to happen, but it seldom does.

The question posed for me was an immediate challenge to assess what I was wanting or what were my future intentions. I became very aware that if one is not wanting to move forward, then they are likely to slip behind. My immediate answer was to answer the question with, 'What's next?' and this book becomes a part of that answer.

Answers do not always require a book to be written, but certainly, some tangible aim should be envisaged, and then work can go towards that aim or goal. Goals will be discussed in greater detail later and become a vital part of one's answer to the question or response to the command.

How many people reach a certain stage in life but have no further goal or objective or purpose other than to randomly accept what comes along? I came across many professional people who have reached a high level of professional achievement but have no further step to achieve.

This could have been true for me—I had gained three degrees, including the PhD, and thought that must be the end of the journey for me at ninety years. But I studied the history of people like Lord Tennyson who at the age of eighty-nine wrote 'Crossing the Bar', an immortal poem; or Caleb, one of the twelve Hebrews to survey the Promised Land of Canaan under the surveillance of Joshua and went ahead and completed the survey successfully for the rest of the Hebrews to enter into the Promised Land; or Michelangelo, who completed the artwork in the Sistine Chapel at an old age.

The truth is if you have no specific direction where you want to go, you may finish up going there—nowhere—where you don't want to go.

This book is written to encourage you to ask the question regularly and truthfully: what's next? It may be the turning point in your life. Don't necessarily always be ready to answer the question, but let it mature in your mind and subconscious to eventually release internal energy to bring the answer.

You may wonder, *Am I a person who can succeed or become more successful than I may be already?* Or conversely, *Have I experienced failure and disappointment in life?* What is success anyway? Is it always getting the right answers or never making a mistake? Sometimes, the wrong answers can lead one on to finding the right answer, or the mistake made can lead to why it was a mistake.

I am reminded of a biblical promise that says, "'For I know the plans I have for you," declares the Lord, "to prosper you and not to harm you, to give you a hope and a future.'" This gives me greater confidence in what I want to gain in life. I have found myself prospering without struggling and have often been surprised at the favour shown to me. This surely is available to others as well as me. This book is to give some of the clues needed to be what is your next or what's next.

For the present, I want you to consider success as achieving what you plan for or gaining something that you are expecting from what you are doing. Very few people with good goals set fail to get good success or results, but those without goals seldom achieve success.

This happens to us all at some time, but it is what we do with the result that will make the difference. I think of the example of Thomas Edison, an inventor, in designing the light bulb. He had so many failures but treated them as events that would not be useful for the light bulb to work. Eventually, he gained the result he was wanting. He didn't give up.

You may be thinking, *Where do I start?* This next chapter will get you thinking of what target you want to reach or aim at or what objectives will take you to your target area. It is amazing how many people just ramble on randomly, hoping for inspiration.

Your background can have a great influence on what you think or plan to do. If you have not had much success in life, then you may not think that you are capable of success and therefore just randomly carry on with little regard to further success and just hope for something better to emerge. The past is the past, and although it may have some influence, the effects can be reduced or overcome.

The present is an important time to overcome the past. In my case, my schooling was severely affected by World War II in which very little schooling was achieved due to constant air raids and bombs falling close by in my neighbourhood. As a result, I gained no school qualifications that would enable me to progress to a further qualification, but this didn't mean that I could not gain a further qualification. If I could change my attitude, then I could change my destiny from one who couldn't to one who could. It sounded so easy if I could only find the best way, and this is what I was determined to do. The results up to this stage confirm the success that started to come my way.

The change in my thinking was a major factor in changing my attitude. This was not just a belief in the power of positive thinking, although that can be very effective in changing my affirmations about success and failure. It seemed that a new sense of success possibilities was replacing the previous attitude of lack of achievement to one of the possibility of gaining any lost time of the past. It truly was a question for me—what's next?—which gave me a new quest for achievement. This can be for anyone prepared to ask that question and act upon it. 'Where the mind goes, man will follow' is a saying which has much truth attached to it and agrees with the opening heading for this chapter.

Chapter 2

Aims, Goals, or Objectives

**Aim for the sky and hit the top the tree. Aim for
the top of the tree and hit the ground.**

Each of these terms may show some intention of where you may
be wanting to go to. A goal is the final point you are wanting to gain,
such as the bullseye on a target. And to accomplish this, an aim is
determined, which may be more specific than the goal. In the case of
the example given, you may be concentrating your aim on the centre
portion of the bullseye rather than the whole of the bullseye.

People who have goals usually have a greater sense of direction and
know where they want to go. Therefore, seek to discover the goals that
are realistic for you, and be prepared to wait for them to occur. This
aspect is well known within the business world and has brought much
success. It is estimated that about 50 per cent of people do not know
where they are going but just randomly get on with life hoping that
good things will result.

Objectives are different to goals in that they tend to be immediately
worked on rather than long-term. They are the starting points that
progressively lead to the goal being reached. For example, if my goal was

5

to become a PhD, then the objectives would be to first gain good degree results that would lead on to the next stage. This is something that the writer is familiar with, for he had not even gained a matriculation to go to university yet wanted to become a PhD. So the first objective was to get a matriculation and then progress from there. The progressive stages may be considered as sub-goals. The result for me—the goal was achieved.

Generally, goals are statements made by a person indicating something they want to achieve, usually within a certain time frame. They need to be realistic and understandable to the person setting the goal; otherwise, it will be unlikely to be achieved. You may wonder why your goals may be different or the same as someone else. It is because we are not all the same but different in individuality or characteristics. This will be covered more specifically in a later chapter on individuality.

A goal, if carefully set, can be the means of motivating you. It may be that there is no motivation without a goal because it is the driving force behind what you are doing or wanting to do. Ask yourself what your goal or goals are. You will be surprised to find that you may not be able to answer positively and wonder why you may be lacking in motivation.

Be flexible enough to change or modify your goals, particularly if you see that there does not appear to be much progress made to achieve them. Sometimes, goals may be too difficult or too far into the future ahead for certain individual types, and therefore, they may let go of them before they materialise. As long as the goal is kept alive, it will produce results. Have a close look at how to design or set up our own programme. This one shown was successful for one student and is why it is given in this book.

You will notice where objectives and aims are in the goal strategy. They are found within the lesson sub-goals. Get those established early on in your goal construction, and the rest will fit in comfortably.

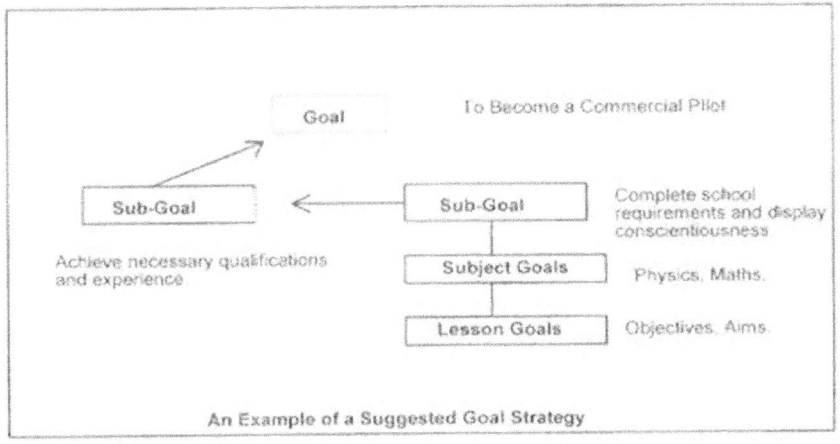

An Example of a Suggested Goal Strategy

Important Points in Goal Construction

- The goal needs to be specific, measurable, attainable, and realistic.
- Benefits from the goal need to be clearly understood by you.
- Possible obstacles and solutions to your goals need to be recognised.
- Specific action steps and time frame for achieving your goals need to be stated.

One vital point regarding goals is to speak them to yourself regularly as well as writing them down so that they are continually before you. If the goal is not regularly kept alive, it will gradually lose its power as a goal. Goals therefore become charged statements rather like words and will produce actions as long as you hold on to them without wavering.

You may be saying to yourself, 'What's next?' That is a good question that may be answered in this book, but it is more essential that you have the answer yourself at this stage. Continually be looking for the answer within this book.

Chapter 3

Discover Your Individuality Type 'You are unique....'

You may have observed that you are not the same as someone else or even like the same things. This is because each one of us is unique although we may have some features similar to someone else. You may have found that you may even prefer a different way of learning things to someone else. Our individuality can be recognised by a several distinctive features: how you prefer to take in knowledge or learn, and how you prefer to act upon that knowledge. These two functions make up what is called a functional pair. They make up a sequence called an individuality type.[1,3.]

In this section you will be able to find out aspects about your individuality, sometimes called personality, that will enable you to understand yourself better and also to understand other people. There are various instruments such as questionnaires used to identify individuality with some more useful than others. Any analysis programs needs to be reliable, that is if you do it a second or third time you will come out with similar results. The one that is used in this book is a very reliable one and not too complicated to use.

Important aspects of individuality useful for you to know are; How do you tend to direct your energy - is it inwardly towards ideas, or outwardly toward people? How do you prefer to take in knowledge or information, and how do you tend make decisions upon the knowledge you have gained?

Each of these aspects can be crucial in deciding 'what is next'. Don't be alarmed if someone else may have a different attitude than you, it is usually because they may be a different personality type. What is important for you that you find out some essential elements about you. You are not the same as someone else although you may have some similar characteristics or traits.You may think like or act like them, but there will difference found in the other parts of your personality. I am a teacher, but we do not all think alike or choose the same subject we teach.

A modified Form of Questionnaire based upon the ideas of Myers-Briggs was constructed by G.Lawrence.2. I have used and redeveloped this questionnaire, with some adjustments to provide a quick approximation of personality type within the criteria used by Myers-Briggs.[1,3]

INDIVIDUAL TYPE QUESTIONNAIRE

The following questionnaire will enable you to study your self in some of the ways you think and act.There are no right or wrong patterns. Think carefully and try to choose the answer that really describes you best. The exercise is not a test. It is simply a way to start looking at the patters in yourself.[3]

INSTRUCTIONS Place a tick on the line alongside the statement that best describes you, for each of the following pair of statements (ONLY ONE TICK ALLOWED FOR EACH PAIR OF STATEMENTS)

(A)

I like learning activities with much activity and variety.	I like quietness for learning and time to consider things.
I like to study by talking through problems with other students.	I like to study and learn on my own before talking and sharing with other students.
I act quickly to solve problems and schoolwork without much thought or reflection.	I am usually slow to start on schoolwork and learning tasks because I need to give much thought to what is required.
I like to see how other people do a job and to see their results so that it may help me with similar tasks.	I like to understand the idea of and to work alone or with just a few people to solve and with learning problems.
I want to know from others what standards of work are required.	I like to set my own standards.

(B)

I prefer to learn from practical experience.	I like to understand the meaning of facts and how they fit together.
I like to use my senses (eyes, ears,touch, taste, and smell) to improve my understanding of things.	I like to use my imagination to come up with new ways to do things or find new possibilities.
I dislike solving new learning problems unless I fully understand ways to solve them.	I like solving new problems and discovering new ways to do things.
I enjoy using skills already learned more than learning new ones.	I like learning new skills more than practising old ones.
I am patient with details and like the challenge of complicated learning tasks.	I dislike complicated learning tasks and may become impatient if details are complicated.

(C)

I like to make decisions logically and based on facts.	I like to decide things based on personal feelings and human values, even if they are not logical.
I like to be treated fairly and without favouritism.	I like to be praised and to please people, even in unimportant things.
I may neglect and hurt other people's feelings without knowing it.	I am aware of other people's feelings and try not to hurt them.
I give more attention to ideas or things than to human relationships.	I am more sensitive to how others feel than with ideas.
I do not easily get upset by arguments.	I get upset by arguments and conflicts.

(D)

I like to have a plan, to have things settled and decide ahead.	I like to stay flexible and avoid fixed plans.
I try to make things come out the way they 'ought to be'.	I deal easily with unexpected happenings.
I like to finish one project before starting on another.	I like to start many projects but may have trouble finishing them all.
I usually have my mind made up.	I am often undecided and in need of more information.
I want to be right.	I do not want to miss anything.
I live by standards and schedules that are not easily changed.	I live by standards and schedules that can be changed to deal with problems as they arise.
I tend to decide things quickly.	I do not want to miss anything.

RESULTS. (Add up your tick responses for each of the following sections)

A. LEFT_____   RIGHT_____

B. LEFT_____   RIGHT_____

C. LEFT_____   RIGHT_____

D. LEFT_____   RIGHT_____

Thank you for your cooperation.

INDIVIDUAL TYPING - PATTERNS ₃

Shade each of the boxes below with the scores gained from your Individual Type questionnaire. These boxes relate to the results given in A. B. C. and D.

This will show you the extent of each scale. For example, if you gained 3 in extroversion and 2 for introversion in section A, this indicates that you vary between extroversion and introversion, but may at times be more inclined to direct your energy outwards towards people than inwards towards ideas, although you may find yourself occasionally being concerned with ideas.

Similar the results within each of the other boxes will indicate extent of each scale. There is no right or wrong pattern for these boxes but they will show you something about how you think and make decisions, It is rare a person to have 5 score for a scale, or a 7 for the 'D' scale but it would not be abnormal.

Chapter 1

As a man thinks, so is he.
Proverbs 23:7

In order to change one's lifestyle, it is vital that one changes their thinking. Thinking occurs in the mind and is necessary to cause changes to affect one's actions. Just how to change one's thinking will be covered in more detail later, but keep in mind that it can have a great effect upon your response to the question posed in the title of this book.

The question, command, prediction, or prophecy 'what's next?' can be either or all and can have a tremendous effect on your destiny, but it depends upon what you do with it. It may depend upon whether you ask the question of yourself or whether someone asks the question for you.

In many cases, people may not be aware of what is likely to happen next or may not be thinking about the possibilities of being able to influence what will be next for them. But this book will provide ideas to cause you to determine what you would like to happen next so as to avoid random consequences or even no further planned happenings occurring in your life. Why not pursue a positive direction for your life by making positive choices and developing goals for your life? This is what I had decided, and you may read about one of the positive consequences for me.

Having completed my PhD at the age of seventy and then published my first book at the age of eighty-seven, I was asked by a news reporter, 'What's next?' This is a question that may be the name for the next TV program, but it could be an indicator of where you are or where you may be wanting to proceed to in life or what is it that you may be wanting to do, such as develop a new project or invention. It basically is a question as to what you are wanting to do or be. Without it, you may be wandering around quite aimlessly or randomly expecting the good to happen, but it seldom does.

The question posed for me was an immediate challenge to assess what I was wanting or what were my future intentions. I became very aware that if one is not wanting to move forward, then they are likely to slip behind. My immediate answer was to answer the question with, 'What's next?' and this book becomes a part of that answer.

Answers do not always require a book to be written, but certainly, some tangible aim should be envisaged, and then work can go towards that aim or goal. Goals will be discussed in greater detail later and become a vital part of one's answer to the question or response to the command.

How many people reach a certain stage in life but have no further goal or objective or purpose other than to randomly accept what comes along? I came across many professional people who have reached a high level of professional achievement but have no further step to achieve.

This could have been true for me—I had gained three degrees, including the PhD, and thought that must be the end of the journey for me at ninety years. But I studied the history of people like Lord Tennyson who at the age of eighty-nine wrote 'Crossing the Bar', an immortal poem; or Caleb, one of the twelve Hebrews to survey the Promised Land of Canaan under the surveillance of Joshua and went ahead and completed the survey successfully for the rest of the Hebrews to enter into the Promised Land; or Michelangelo, who completed the artwork in the Sistine Chapel at an old age.

The truth is if you have no specific direction where you want to go, you may finish up going there—nowhere—where you don't want to go.

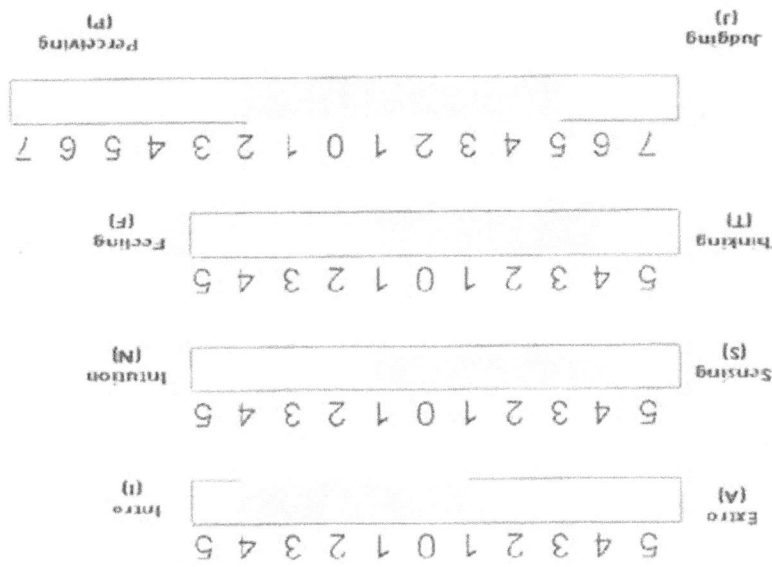

Completing Your Pattern

Now that you have completed the questionnaire you can construct your own box diagram and shade in your 'IndividualType' - Pattern, similar to the following diagram but with your scores. This diagram shows my results, indicating I am an ISTJ type. You will notice these boxes relate in order to the responses given in A, B, C, and D. This will show you the extent of each scale.

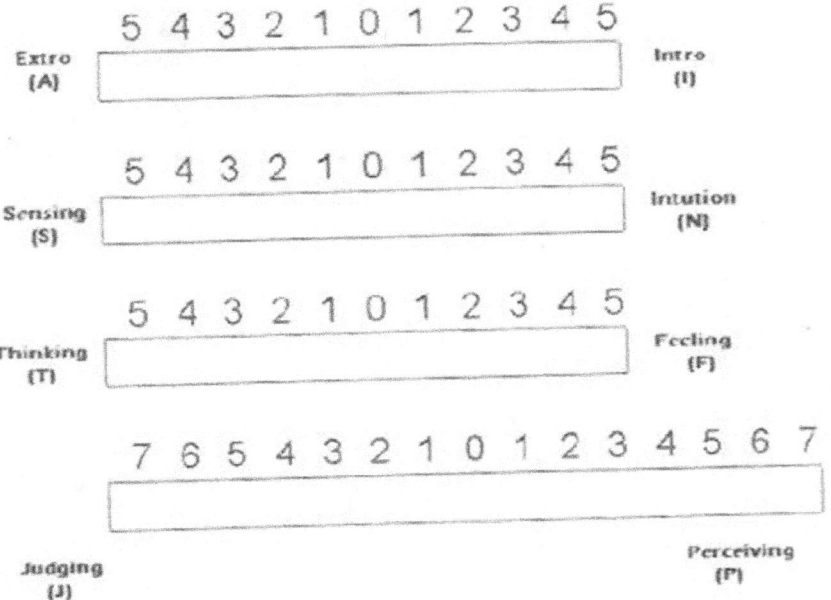

This diagram shows the results gained by an ISTJ Type

Details of the characteristics of your type can be found in the Notes section in this book.

Chapter 4

Attitude and Thinking

Where the mind goes, man follows.

This chapter contains one of the most important principles to achieve an answer to, what's next? These two factors of attitude and thinking are closely related to each other.

Attitude are the thoughts that you have towards something. These may be positive or negative. Both will produce a result. If one has the attitude that he or she can succeed, then the mind is in a state to achieve what one is trying for. Similarly, if the attitude is that one cannot do something, then that is the likely result.

We have found that achievement is directly related to a form of motivation called achievement motivation.[4] A good attitude toward achievement will produce higher achievement.[3,7] So you need to find out what gives you a good attitude.

Well, it simply comes from your thinking or your thoughts. It was Henry Ford who said, 'If you think you can or think you can't, you are right.' Therefore, simply change your thinking and change your attitude. But is it as simple as this?

Our thoughts come from many sources: our backgrounds, former experiences or learning, our social groups or status, our socioeconomic group, religion, or ideals that we may have formed in our minds or words that we have spoken. Each one of those elements can have a strong effect upon attitude.

Words are very powerful tools to change our attitude. Even the Bible tells us much about words: that we 'shall eat the fruit of our words' or 'bring life or death'. There is another strong principle relating to words that will not be covered at this point other than to state that they are very important for changing your attitude.

Here is an analogy to convince you that by changing an attitude, you can change position. An aircraft flying in level flight can either climb or dive under the control of the pilot. This is able to be done by elevators fixed to the tail of the aircraft. Put in one position, the aircraft will climb, and put in another position, it will dive. What causes the aircraft to change its position? It is the elevators being used to change the attitude under control of the pilot.

A similar phenomena occurs with our attitude. We do not have elevators to have to be changed but motivators that need to be activated. Good motivators can cause us to climb higher with greater achievement or dive lower with underachievement.[3,7]

These good motivators can be words, results, value, expectation, incentive, and worth, to mention some major ones. More specifics on motivation will come later, but without motivation, success is limited.

There is another form of motivation related to this principle of using effective words, and it is called attributional motivation.[5,7]

By using a form of attributional training, improved learning will occur.[6] So your answer to the 'What's next?' question can be stated in clear terms audibly to oneself or to others. But you will need to believe that what you say will occur.

THINKING

Now to say something about thinking. It is something that goes on in the brain and can strongly influence one's actions.

Our thinking mainly results from our talking or words that we use. So if we want to change our attitude and actions leading to greater achievement, we need to be watching what words we use.

Positive words tend to produce positive actions and results, and negative words the opposite., It is the words that we use that determine our thinking and the attitude that results from our thinking. It is not that our thinking changes the words we use, but vice versa. So the secret to change one's thinking is by changing the words that we use.

Such phrases as 'I can do this' or 'I will be able to achieve this' enter the subconscious and cause the person to do what they say. Again, this is a biblical principle of saying what one believes.

There have been a number of distinct thinking styles identified by Professor Anthony Gregore at the University of Connecticut and they are:[8]

- concrete random (CRT)
- abstract random (ART)
- abstract sequential (AST)
- concrete sequential (CST)

A brief description of these four styles is given here to show that we do not all think in the same way.

Concrete sequential thinkers (CST) are based upon reality. They process information in an ordered, sequential way. To them, reality consists of what they can detect through their physical senses: sight, touch, sound, taste, and smell. They remember facts, specific information, and rules with ease. If you are a concrete sequential thinker, build on your strengths. Provide yourself with details, and break your projects down into specific steps.[8]

Concrete random thinkers (CRT) are based upon reality and tend to take a trial-and-error approach. Because of this, they may take intuitive leaps for true creative thought. They have a strong trend to find alternatives and do things in their own way. They tend to see things from more than one viewpoint. Put yourself in a position to solve problems.[8]

Abstract random thinkers (ART) operate in the world of feelings and emotions. They absorb ideas and information and organise them through reflection. They remember best if information is personalised. They may feel restricted when they are subject to a very structured environment. They need to look at the big picture first and allow enough time to finish the job. The use of visual clues is very helpful.8

Abstract sequential thinkers (AST) like the world of theory and abstract thought. They like to think in concepts and analyse information. They may like philosophy and research. They can easily zoom on anything which is important, such as key points and significant details. Their thinking is logical, rational, and intellectual, like reading and research. Generally, they prefer to work alone.

The following Chart 1 may help you to analyse your thinking style.8

To test your own thinking style, read each set of words and mark the two that best describe you.

Chart 1

1. a. imaginative
    b. investigative
    c. realistic
    d. analytical

2. a. organised
    b. adaptable
    c. critical
    d. inquisitive

3. a. debating
    b. getting to the point
    c. creating
    d. relating

9. a. reader
    b. people person
    c. problem-solver
    d. planner

10. a. memorise
    b. associate
    c. think through
    d. originate

11. a. changer
    b. judger
    c. spontaneous
    d. wants direction

4. a. personal
    b. practical
    c. academic
    d. adventurous

5. a. precise
    b. flexible
    c. systematic
    d. inventive

6. a. sharing
    b. orderly
    c. sensible
    d. independent

7. a. competitive
    b. perfectionist
    c. cooperative
    d. logical

8. a. intellectual
    b. sensitive
    c. hard-working
    d. risk-taking

12. a. communicating
    b. discovering
    c. cautious
    d. reasoning

13. a. challenging
    b. practicing
    c. caring
    d. examining

14. a. completing work
    b. seeing possibilities
    c. gaining ideas
    d. interpreting

15. a. doing
    b. feeling
    c. thinking
    d. experimenting

After completing the test, place your results in the columns below in the following Chart 2. Circle the letters of the words you chose for each number in the previous chart. Add the totals for Columns I, II, III, and IV. Multiply the total of each columns by 4. The box with the highest number describes how you most often process information.

Chart 2

	I	II	III	IV
1.	C	D	A	B
2.	A	C	B	D
3.	B	A	D	C
4.	B	C	A	D
5.	A	C	B	D
6.	B	C	A	D
7.	B	D	C	A
8.	C	A	B	D
9	D	A	B	C
10	A	C	B	D
11	D	B	C	A
12	C	D	A	B
13	B	D	C	A
14	A	C	D	B
15	A	C	B	D

TOTAL

Chart 2—cont.

I   _____   × 4   =   _____   Concrete Sequential (CS)

II   _____   × 4   =   _____   Abstract Sequential (AS)

III   _____   × 4   =   _____   Abstract Random (AR)

IV   _____   × 4   =   _____   Concrete Random (CR)

Chapter 5

Motivation—that which causes you to start or stop something or keep on doing it.

Have you ever wondered what makes you want to do something yet at other times may not be interested in doing something similar? Also, you may find that you do not like doing something that other people may like doing. Well, it is something that is called motivation, and this may not be quite the same for all people. During research, I found that this inner driving force is related to individuality: that is, that certain individuality types may be motivated more easily than others. This driving force can be influenced by outside influences, such as by others and also by events and personal desire.

Whatever your 'What's next?' is will require some force or power to achieve. This may be directed towards an idea or a personal desire or passion or to a question or to a personal goal. Just having a goal or a vision will not be sufficient to achieve what you are wanting. Action will also be needed, and this is where a force called a motivating force is required. Marilyn King, an Olympic athlete, said, 'Passion + vision + action is the equation for success.'[8]

This strong force that originates within you that can cause you to achieve what you set your heart on is called motivation, coming from the Latin meaning 'to cause to move'. I defined this to be 'the internal release of energy to accomplish some desired result'. It is suggested that there may well be two forces at work in motivation: a pulling from without and a pushing from within. If these two forces are working in the same direction, maximum result of movement may be achieved. The pulling from without can be visualised as encouragement supplied by others, such as teachers, parents, or friends, and that from within is from a motivation centre within the brainstem that is activated to release energy. Imagine this action as rather like a switch being turned on or off. You are either motivated or not motivated. To get the best results from your intention requires the switch to be turned on.

An important thing about motivation is that we are not all motivated by the same things or to the same extent. Different individuality or personality types may be motivated by different causes and ways of thinking. Now that you know your type, you will see various ways in which you can be motivated or increase your motivation.

Within this chapter, I will explain what is needed to increase your motivation and factors that may decrease it. A lack of motivation is a major cause of underachievement. This can be a problem for all people at various times during their lives, but any serious consequences may be avoided or removed by knowing what can be done to increase motivation.

In my particular history, I could have been very lacking in motivation, for I had left school not having gained any educational qualification whatsoever because my schooling was affected during World War II. But I was later to go to three universities in three different countries, finally gaining a PhD. It was motivation that became a major factor in my success. Was this some miracle or a rarity? No. I was later to be a secondary school teacher, gaining much success with very low-stream students at national examinations. I proved the point that if the motivation level could be increased, then achievement could be increased.

Most definitions of motivation include statements or infer that motivation consists of three basic components that may activate, direct, and sustain human behaviour.

Activating forces or pressures are assumed to exist within a person, which may cause them to behave or act within a person. This may cause them to behave or act in certain ways. The activating force may start an action or may stop an action—this leads to the possibility of negative motivation. It is possible to misinterpret a lack of motivation as the cause of underachievement, but it may be a high form of motivation to avoid success. The action of stopping something is not always negative but can be positive and still require a motivation force to stop whatever is being done.

The essential components of motivation are:

- *goal* in order to have in you a desired result or position to be achieved
- *expectation* in order to have a high expectation of your goal being realised
- *value* in order to see your desired goal as being worthwhile and valuable
- *self-concept* in order to see yourself capable of reaching your goal.

Each of these components is essential to give a sufficient motivating force for whatever is desired. Here is an example of an equation showing the combined effect each of the components has.

$$E(g + v + sc)$$

E. = expectation, g = goal, v = value, sc = self-concept.

If we have a score of 1–10 for g, v, and sc, it would equal 30. This total would now be multiplied by the value of E. So if E was 1, the product would be 30. But by increasing the E, the product increases greatly. Just by increasing E to 2, the total now becomes 60 or double what it was. What this example reinforces is the value of having a high level of expectation.

In an experience I had with two low-ability classes, I asked them at the start of the year how many would like to pass a national exam. They all put their hands up, indicating they wanted to pass, but when asked if they expected to pass, not one hand was raised. We had a problem because if the E was 0, then there was insufficient motivating force to achieve what they wanted. But there was a way around it for me because I was able to replace their expectation with mine for them. The result—most passed the exam at the end of the year. Their motivation had been raised to change their attitude of not believing they could to that of believing that they would pass. It was not quite as easy as this, for other factors had to be used to maintain good motivation throughout the year.

There are two distinct approaches to motivation: the content approach and the process approach. From time to time, these two approaches may be combined. The content approach specifies only what things motivate behaviour, such as achievement, appreciation, food when hungry, and money. When these are supplied, a person becomes more motivated.

The second approach is the process type, involving the behaviour processes and how behaviour is started and modified. This approach includes expectancy theory, goal theory, and attributional theory. Within this process approach, there are two types of motivation, which this book mainly deals with. They are technically known as achievement motivation and attributional motivation.[4,5,6,8]

Achievement Motivation

This includes all the aspects of behaviour that cause a person to become activated towards achievement. Several factors contribute to achievement motivation and technically are called causal factors. One of these causal factors emphasises the environmental factors that affect statements made relating to achievement, which are called attributions. For example, if another person informs someone else that he or she lacks the ability or is lazy, then an attribution may be formed based upon someone else's opinion. This can form an attitude within the person affected by the attribution. This can apply to both positive and negative attributions. To be told that you are doing good will create a positive attribution and improve achievement motivation.

Similarly, the attitude one has towards learning or towards some task will affect this form of motivation, towards either success or failure.

The second factor that affects this form of motivation is the attitude the person has towards learning as well as the view they have of themselves or self-concept. This will depend much on how much a person understands the situation and able to interpret events within the situation and be able to process information about the situation.[6,7] One will need to have a good attitude or reason for learning or doing something as well as knowing what is required to complete the task. When both of these factors are high, the achievement is also high.

There are three general components of a person's motivation beliefs that considerably affect the statements or attributions associated with the performance. These are expectancy or expectation, the value of what is being attempted, and the effect or the way a person feels from such action.

Achievement motivation is largely influenced by the statements or attributions made by a person and become the basis behind another type of motivation called attributional motivation.

The important factors that contribute towards achievement motivation are:

1. Recognising that something is worthwhile.
2. Success can be expected from what you decide to do.
3. Having a goal or the desired result.
4. Seeing yourself capable of achieving your goal.

Attributional Motivation

This is a form of motivation that results from the statements (attributions) you or others make on reasons for success or failure. Therefore, motivation may be high or low depending on the attributions made. Sometimes, even a failure can increase motivation if one realises that with a different strategy, success was possible. Even success does not always improve motivation, but it could be a good incentive for future success.[9] It is believed by some theorists that by identifying the cause or reason for a particular outcome, it may be possible to find out psychological consequences and therefore make attributions that can change the situation. A good approach for this type of motivation is to search for an understanding of why an event has occurred. This may be especially for a failure. This 'spring of action' is a central assumption behind this form of motivation.[9]

Attributions may more easily change the thought processes than for the thought processes to change the attributions. Therefore, verbal attributions are a vital link for achievement motivation and become important relating to the type of thoughts and statement you make. The thoughts are the inaudible or silent words or mental pictures that enter the mind consciously or unconsciously. This can affect the self-image a person may have of themselves and thereby affect their achievement motivation.

It has been mentioned before but is worth repeating: 'Audible words will change one's thinking and therefore change one's attitude.' It is this factor that makes attributional motivation effective, using such statements as these for success: 'My success has resulted from my efforts and a good strategy.' For failures, this type of statement can be used: 'With a better strategy, I will master these type of problems and improve my results.'

Now you have the secrets of how to realise your 'what's next'.

Chapter 6

Getting Started

What to Do Now!

Once you have asked yourself some questions such as what do I want to do now? or where do I go from here? you can start to build up a picture profile either in your mind or written on paper. Establish your goals first, then decide on what objectives will take you to your goals.

Remember the power that comes from your audible words to yourself. These will help you to change or establish your thinking about the goals you are seeking. You will find that your motivation will grow stronger as you accomplish the objectives you are using to reach your goals.

You must hold on to your goals without wavering and keep them alive by using regular attribution statements concerning them, such as 'I am improving my understanding of this problem' or 'My knowledge is increasing as I learn new things.' Sharing your knowledge or exhibiting your knowledge to others can increase your motivation. Therefore, motivation is a major requirement for your 'what's next' project. When your first project is completed, then look forward to the next one. This will enable you to make continual progress and lead you on to greater fulfilment and satisfaction.

Keep a record of your goals and any things that will undermine them or take your mind off them. Without a goal, there will be no motivation, and therefore, a failure will likely occur. Therefore, goals are going to be your main factor in dealing with what's next. You are now in a position to move on with confidence, recognising your individuality and what is needed to accomplish what you can set your mind on: 'As a man thinks, so is he.' Your thinking starts from the words that you use, and your attitude is changed mainly by your thinking.

Chapter 7

The Way Ahead Is Clear
. . . What's Next?

This book intends to give you a clear way to answer such a statement as, what is next? It is amazing how often you may hear this statement or think of it. You may get into the habit of asking the question for yourself, which is a positive way of moving ahead and preventing you from getting into a rut and randomly going through life without a realistic aim.

A major emphasis in this book is related to the uniqueness of your individuality or personality and the attitudes you use to adapt to life's challenges. You are not exactly like someone else, but you are you. The more you can know about yourself, the better you will be to give a positive answer to the 'what's next' situation.

This could be in the area of your occupational choice and finding what would be best for you to gain greater satisfaction and reward. It may not always be easy to change whatever job you are currently doing, which may not be suitable for your type but sufficient to keep a roof over your head and food on the table. Therefore, don't just throw it away but use it as a stepping stone to go on further.

This book shows what determines your attitude and how one can change it by changing one's thinking. This is a secret regarding attitude. The words you use determine your thinking, so from this moment on, be careful with the words you use because that is what your thinking will be related to.

Motivation has been stressed as being a prerequisite for success, so keep this in mind to always see a good result coming from your decision-making and maintain a high level of expectation. Speak positive affirmations audibly to yourself, for this will influence your subconscious state, for it is from 'the fruit of your mouth you will be satisfied'. Again, you can see the influence that words will have upon your attitude. 'You can' rather than 'You can't.' Either of these statements requires the same amount of energy and effort to do, but the result is considerably different.

You are now ready and equipped to answer your 'what's next?' or decide what it will be.

References

1. Briggs-myers, I & Briggs, P (1992) Gifts Differing. Consulting Psychological Palo Alto. CA:Press, Inc.
2. Lawrence G. (1982) <u>People, types and tiger stripes.</u> Gainesville, FI. Centre for Application of Psychological Type Inc.
3. Restall L.J. (2016) <u>'In Pursuit of Success – Overcoming Underachievement'</u>, Xlibris.co.nz
4. Adelman H.S. & Taylor (1993). <u>Learning problems and learning disabilities:Moving forward.</u> California: Brooks/ Cole Publishing Company.
5. Weiner, B. (undated). Attributional theory, achievement motivation, and the educational process. <u>Review of Educational Research, 42,</u> (2), 203-214.
6. Borowski, J.G Weyhing, R.S. Carr, M. (1988). Effects of attributional training on strategy-based reading comprehension in learning-disabled students. <u>Journal of Educational Psychology, 80,</u> (91), 46-53.
7. Weiner, B. & Kukla, A.(1970b), An attributional analysis of achievement motivation. <u>Journal of Personality and Social Psychology, 15,</u> (1), 1-20.
8. Dryden, D. & Voss, J, (1993). <u>The Learning Revolution Profile Books</u>. Hong Kong.355-359.
9. Weiner, B. (1979). A theory of motivation for some classroom experiences. <u>Journal of Educational Psychology.</u> 71 (1).

About the Author

The author has gained three university degrees, including a PhD. Either he seems to have it made for him or he is brilliant, lucky, or have lived in a time or place where achievements were easy to obtain. This is far from the truth, and the following account of his life up to the present time should be an encouragement for you, particularly if you do not have a record of success.

I was born in London to good and loving parents and lived most of my childhood in Essex, an eastern part of London. My schooling, or lack of it, during World War II was completed under conditions in which very little learning was accomplished. Most of us wondered and were more concerned as to whether we would be alive at the end of the day.

My experience was like this: on most days, no sooner had I arrived at school, the air raid siren would sound, and we were hounded into makeshift shelters, often without any books or learning material, and sit it out with our hearts' inner mouths. I cannot remember anything that was taught during those times. Our teachers who would read to us and take our minds off the bombs that were falling around encouraged us, but the normal lessons were not given.

At seventeen years and six months, in 1946, I joined the RAF (Royal Air Force) as a trainee to become a physical training instructor, eventually to be retained as a staff instructor on the training school. It was there that my learning desire took root and is still with me to this day at the age of ninety-one. Some would say that it is was because I was the type made for learning and that my ability lay dormant in me and was just waiting to get out. 'Second chance must not mean second best' is a truth that means much to me and can be for anyone who believes it and acts on it. What could be the reason for this change, and how was I to catch up with the many years lost during my schooling?

I later transferred into the Royal New Zealand Air Force, employed in a similar role training other instructors for the combined services, army, navy, and air force in physical fitness. My pursuit or passion for learning was intense. I attended education classes and passed a higher educational test, similar to a school certificate, and gained an associateship by examination with the New Zealand Association of Health, Physical Education, and Recreation (NZAHPER), the first of several professional examinations I was to pass.

One of the outstanding principles I acquired during my air force service was the importance of motivation, which I was first introduced to in 1947 and has stayed with me and increased in intensity since those days. It became major for me during my master of education degree in1995 and has convinced me that it is a vital element in achieving anything worthwhile.

When I left the air force, I went to Saint Luke's College, the University of Exeter, to complete a certificate of education. I then went on to teach in a secondary school in England before transferring back to a New Zealand secondary school for the next twenty years.

I completed a bachelor of education degree and a master of education degree in New Zealand and, from the result of my master's degree, was given a grant free access to complete a doctor of philosophy degree in Western Australia in1999. This gave me three degrees from three different countries: England, New Zealand, and Australia. Many parts of my degree training were in the area of education for gifted students, learning difficulties, and individuality in education. I later wrote and published a book, *In Pursuit of Success: Overcoming Underachievement*. It was from this book that I had the inspiration to write a companion book called *What's Next*. This applied directly to me, but I then realised it can apply to anyone, for it is not only a surprise statement but also can be questioned to me or someone else to me. Therefore, I did have an answer to what's next.

You may have gathered already that passion and motivation were strong components in my success story. This is true, but success does not need to be just arriving at a place or time in life or gaining some particular experience or qualification but can be a journey of discovery, adventure, or excitement throughout life. The pursuit of success can be considered to be proof of one's desire. If your desire is strong, then you will pursue that desire strongly. In looking back, I can see that I had a strong desire to achieve. Nothing could be more frustrating than to have reached one's personal goals and then stop—what's next? Life is a continual journey with exciting prospects on the way. One success should be the stepping stone to another one. Let this account stir you on to discover what is next.